BRAIN GONE WILD

A TALE OF ELECTRODES SCHIZOPHRENIA AND JOHN

By Polly deButts

Foreword by
E. Fuller Torrey

The opinions expressed in this manuscript are solely the opinions of the author and do not represent the opinions or thoughts of the publisher. The author has represented and warranted full ownership and/or legal right to publish all the materials in this book.

Brain Gone Wild
A Tale of Electrodes, Schizophrenia, and John

v2.0

Outskirts Press, Inc.
http://www.outskirtspress.com

ISBN: 978-1-4787-2969-3

PRINTED IN THE UNITED STATES OF AMERICA

THIS BOOK IS DEDICATED TO JOHN
FOR HIS FRANTIC EFFORTS IN DEALING WITH A
"BRAIN GONE WILD"
AND HIS VALIANT ATTEMPTS TO UNDERSTAND
WHY HIS LIFE IS STILL
A MYSTERY TODAY

Table of Contents

FOREWORD

This is a brief and well-written account by a mother who has spent more than a quarter century helping her son manage his schizophrenia illness. For such parents, and there are many of them, schizophrenia is not merely a family Illness, it becomes a life career. The story is typical in many ways, including the struggles of the son, intermittent medication noncompliance, substance abuse, and many small victories for both mother and son which make the struggle worthwhile. Ms. deButts writes with compassion and a sense of humor. Readers may not agree with all of her decisions regarding how to respond to her son's substance abuse, but will admire her efforts to keep her son afloat during the worst storms. Especially valuable in the book is her "Memo to Parents from a Schizophrenic Son." I recommend Ms. deButts' book as a good read for all families who have a family member afflicted with this perplexing disease.

E. Fuller Torrey, MD
Executive Director of the Stanley Medical Research Institute
Founder of the Treatment Advocacy Center

1 The Present

I STOOD AT the front door and watched him walk away from the house just as it was beginning to snow, a few flakes drifting from the sky. His black knit cap fitting tightly on his head, his upright stance causing his large stomach to protrude, both hands deep into his pockets, he turned and gave his rare smile and said, "Thanks."

What was he thanking me for? A life without meaning? A life in which each day he fights a battle against alien computers attacking his body, al Qaeda agents constantly watching him, and a brain at war with itself, reality versus fantasy?

I waved at my 46-year-old son and said, "Call me later," sighing and thinking to myself as I usually did each day, *what an empty life he leads*. Today, he had spent a few hours doing odd jobs for me around the house.

Half an hour later, my phone rings. It is John. He tells me he is at the Metro Station calling from a pay phone. He wants me to know that as he was leaving my house he saw strange people hanging around and wants me to be very careful and not answer the door without knowing who is there. I told him that Paul, our next-door neighbor, has a small band of musicians and maybe they were strange looking. He said "no, you may think I'm crazy but these are not musicians." OK, I said, and agreed to be careful.

Earlier in the week, John had confided to me that the computer voices were constantly talking to him, saying, "I see him." "Kill him."

"You're gonna die."

He confessed, "It takes all my energy to fight them. I have to, if I agree with them I feel like dying. Here's the thing, any activity takes energy and I hear a voice every two seconds, that's 30 messages a minute coming in ... think about it. You say Brain Disease, so I have a disease. These voices jumped into my injured brain, like injured animals in the wild who are killed and eaten; I'm like that."

He continues, "I hate to tell you this but you know when I felt this bad before... I would get 'street drugs' and they made me feel so much better. But I can't do that now."

"Street Drugs." The very mention of them fills me with terror. Self-medication for a war-torn brain. Dual Diagnosis: psychosis and drug addiction, two co-occurring disorders which beg for understanding and treatment. The federal government estimates that about 7 million adults in the U.S. suffer from these disorders and more than 90 percent are not getting proper treatment.

Hearing John say, "But I can't do that now," referring to street drugs, I listened, I hoped, I prayed for this to be a true statement. Over the years, it has been an ongoing effort to find the right medication for him so that he will not have to medicate himself. But even with the right medication, the alcohol or drug abuse must be addressed and treated. I tried to understand this and not to expect an instant recovery. It is such a long road and with each step forward there are more steps backward.

Later that same day, with the snow still falling, John calls again.

"When I went out for cigarettes I saw some of those strange people. They evidently followed me home. Do you think I should report them to the police?" I protested that if he called the police he would end up in the hospital (again) and suggested that he come back over here and we could talk about it. This seemed to calm him down.

"OK," he said. "I'll call you back if they bother me anymore."

I am recounting this particular day because it was a typical day in the normal cycle of John's illness. The manifestations of schizophrenia are separate and unique to each person, just as our personalities are separate and unique....

2 The Past

DECEMBER 1984: TWENTY nine years ago, sitting in the family group session at George Washington University Hospital, hearing the words, "Your son John had been diagnosed as having a schizophreniform disorder" froze my outward expression while, inside, my emotions were violently beating a path to the surface, eager to erupt. In order to control them, I said calmly, "I'm glad we are able to identify the illness. I can deal with a sickness with a name but I cannot deal with a nameless sickness." I did not know then that the name "schizophrenia" could be likened to cancer, in that there are as many forms of schizophrenia as there are of cancer. To further control my inside emotional tempest and not resort to a loud scream, I even had these outrageous words to say:

"When you know the name of your enemy, you can educate yourself; without a name you would flounder in a quagmire of speculation." Again, I was covering my emotional overload and I knew absolutely nothing about the subject I was discussing.

I looked at John. His eyes were staring blankly at the floor. He looked young and handsome – but vulnerable. His dark brown curly hair was complemented by a beard, which gave him the appearance of one of the early Flemish painters in a deep study. How could this be happening? Why wouldn't I have had some warning or some clue over the nineteen years that John was growing up? He was just as normal during those years as his sister and three brothers; in fact, although he was the youngest, he was often the most serene and tolerant in this vociferous and boisterous group.

The telephone call from Richmond that precipitated this meeting had come six weeks earlier. It was right after Thanksgiving and I was working at my desk at home before dinner. The caller explained that she was a casual friend of John's, and what she told me must have activated all the adrenalin in my body because the loud pounding of my heart made it difficult to hear what she was saying. I remember my hand holding the phone was shaking so badly I had to hold the phone with both hands. The words, "He must have gone into the museum and stolen a painting ... worth a lot of money; and then he gave it to me... he told me he had gotten it at the museum and that it was the most beautiful painting he had ever seen. It has been returned, but I think John needs help – he has done some other strange things lately." I did not wait to hear any more; I asked if she would try to find John and keep him at his apartment until I could get there. Within an hour JHS, (John's stepfather) and I were on the rain-soaked road to Richmond. We stopped several times to call him but there was no answer.

Finally, we connected with him and he said the police had arrested him for trying to break into a motorcycle shop. I was so relieved he was safe, I even thanked God he had attempted burglary. I had feared he would be found dead. We told him we would be in court in the morning when his case was called.

We met him at the courthouse. He smiled at us in a silly manner; it was as if he couldn't stop grinning. His eyes were very bright and he stared at objects around him. He walked as if in a daze, as a sleepwalker might slowly feel his way in a dark room. He was released to our custody under the First Offender treatment.

I brought my attention back to this cheerless room where the entire family was sitting listening to the social worker explaining why John had been diagnosed as having a form of schizophrenia.

"John was initially admitted on November 29, 1984, after being brought to the Emergency Room by you, his parents, because of bizarre behavior. When he was admitted, he exhibited many features consistent with psychosis: withdrawal, frequent inappropriate giggling, evidence of disorganized thinking, delusions and auditory hallucinations. These are probably the best-known symptoms of schizophrenia. We are basing our diagnosis on repeated interviews with John in which he reports that his behavior was in response to auditory hallucinations. Psychological testing concurred. We call John's illness schizophreniform disorder because a true diagnosis is made in part by the course of time. Any questions?"

ANY QUESTIONS? I thought of what I'd like to ask if the social worker felt like spending the next week with me. I had so many questions I did not know where to begin. I heard her saying,

"If there are no questions, it's time for this session to end. We will meet again next week, same time, same place."

I looked at the rest of the family. Were they as stunned at the news as I was? What were they thinking? My son Henry, the eldest, Mary, my daughter, herself a new mother, Tom and Read, almost close enough in age to be twins; all ambitious young adults with growing careers and busy lives – but they always had time for each other. Mary's humor rescued us from our outrage upon learning that John had stolen a valuable painting from the museum by pointing out that he exhibited excellent taste in picking one of the finest examples of French art in the 18th century, a Fragonard!

3 Background

AFTER THE MEETING that day, I walked through a park on my way back to the office, repeating the horrible name of this disease. I couldn't even spell the name, much less know anything about it. There was one thought in the back of my mind which gave me a slight feeling of hope: This disease was not fatal... or was it? Questions, I had so many.

I thought back 20 years ago today when John was born at this same hospital. A beautiful, brown-eyed baby pronounced by the family pediatrician to be as healthy and robust as the other four had been. I was so proud. I had always wanted five children. Furthermore, when I was married in 1952, I was expected to stay at home and raise children. In those days if you had a college degree, it was considered an insurance policy against widowhood. The saying was, "Well, everyone should be able to get a job in an emergency, and with a college degree one could always teach." My own reasoning was that if I had to stay at home with one child, I might as well stay at home with several.

In December 1964, after a natural birth, John weighed in at 7 pounds, 14 ounces, a normal baby in every way. Why didn't this disease show itself then? I was to learn later that the truth about schizophrenia, a disease of the brain, is that John was born with a different brain from the brains of his sister and three brothers. This is a fact. He could have had brain damage very early in life, maybe before he was born, even though the manifestation of the disease didn't appear until he was nineteen years old. I also learned that the disease tends to run in families and after searching the family tree, I found an isolated case, a first cousin once removed on John's father's side. I had to look long and hard, because schizophrenia was still being treated similarly to the way cancer was 50 years ago ... you do not speak its NAME!

The questions that bothered me most were: What was the cause of this disease? What caused John to have it and not his siblings? Was he the weakest because he was the last of the five children? Could it have been prevented?

Currently, there are no factual answers about the cause or causes of schizophrenia. There are many theories; perhaps it is genetic, biochemical (use of prescription or street drugs), viral, or nutritional. These are all good theories but there is no proof yet that any one of them is correct. And maybe a combination of the theories is the answer. One theory that finally has been rejected – and rightly so – is that bad parenting causes schizophrenia.

As I walked through the park, I wondered if John's life was over. Would he improve or just be subjected to a life in a mental hospital? I had no answers and I had so many, many questions.

John's growing-up years were marked by an intense interest in the world around him. He really grew up in the woods behind our house. Every moment he and his friends could spare was spent in the woods examining the latest wildlife or water life in the stream. A tree house still perches high up in one of the tall oak trees. One summer, when he was ten years old, he went off to a sailing camp. He won the Best Camper award, as well as Best Archer and Best Sharpshooter. He also did well in school, taking part in a Gifted and Talented program. He would have done better if he hadn't been so easily distracted by his friends, whom he enjoyed immensely.

He was as normal as any child, an average student all through grade school and high school. He read a great deal, mostly about outdoor life, hunting, camping, and fishing. One day, John shot a squirrel with his BB gun in our backyard. He skinned it, stretched the skin on a board to dry, and asked me to cook the meat. He had often been dove hunting out in the country with his brothers, so this was not an unusual incident. The unusual part was that we lived in a county near the city – and who would want to eat a city squirrel?

4 Beginnings of Schizophrenia

WHEN DID I ever have the slightest suspicion that John might be troubled? Perhaps his freshman year at VCU. He came home almost every weekend, but I never thought anything about it. His brother Read had done the same thing during his first college year. John had lived in the same house ever since he was born, and I thought he probably wasn't quite ready to be away for long periods of time.

I did become concerned when I listened to what John had to say as we were driving back from Richmond after his freshman year:

"I think my roommates were out to get me … they liked to gang up on me; it's been a terrible year, and I never want to go back there. Maybe I'm imagining, but that's a bad place to be ..."

Two days later, John complained of severe stomach pains and cramps. I thought it might be an appendicitis attack, but after one hour in the emergency room at George Washington University Hospital, the doctors could find nothing wrong with him. He showed no symptoms of appendicitis other than the pain, and even that was not localized. Since the pain persisted, I decided to get a second opinion. We visited a surgeon who smiled kindly and told us the same thing: there were no symptoms of appendicitis. I asked what he thought the reason could be for so much pain and he said he couldn't answer that. Something was being overlooked. I knew these pains were very real to John.

A few days later, he complained again. I took him to see our family doctor. After a complete physical examination, Dr. Anderson said there was nothing wrong. He did say that perhaps John should be drinking more water because the test on the urine showed that it was cloudy and strong.

Two days later, we were back in our doctor's office. John said the pain would come and go; he was sure he had some sort of infection. Once again, the water-drinking remedy was the prescription.

After two more visits to the doctor, we finally considered counseling. I looked up the name of a psychologist but never made an appointment. I thought of how adolescence to adulthood has strong growing pains with every kind of stress imaginable. Some of John's symptoms seemed like normal teenage and early adult feelings. I had experienced the moodiness, the apathy, the preoccupation with one's body, the vagueness in thoughts, and the belief that people are watching, with my other four children as they were entering adulthood.

I thought that if I just waited a little longer, John would get better. What I was not aware of at the time was that these exaggerations of normal early adult feelings were actually the beginning stage of his schizophrenia.

Another insight that came to me later was that John was searching for answers everywhere. Each trip to the hospital or the doctor for the inexplicable pain was a muted cry for help. It was a last-ditch effort of John's to maintain some self-respect while facing the enormous odds of overwhelming defeat. He knew something was very wrong.

However, John was able to work part-time in his stepfather's law office for a few weeks that summer. I proposed to take him to my mother's little cottage on a barrier island in North Carolina for two weeks where he would have a good rest and regular meals. My mother was shocked when she saw her grandson – now a sullen and morose young man who walked as if he was heavily sedated.

She was positive he was on street drugs. I, too, was frightened by his extreme apathy and his exhaustion. Was he on drugs? We were both afraid he might be suicidal. He slept for the entire two weeks, only appearing for meals, eating heartily, saying nothing, and retreating to his bed. He showed no interest in sailing, normally a favorite sport, nor in fishing, though he had a brand-new rod. I decided I would seek psychiatric help for him as soon as we arrived home. Why hadn't this been apparent to me earlier?

Once again, I never made the appointment with a psychiatrist because a strange thing happened. John got dramatically better. The two weeks at the beach had performed some sort of miracle on his health. He changed from a non-smiling, non-communicative, depressed person into a smiling, talkative, happy young man. We wondered if this would last. He assured us it would, that he did not need to see a psychiatrist, and that whatever had been wrong with him had gone away. He claimed he felt well again.

That same day, as I reached the center of the park and sat down on a bench, I looked at the people walking in front of me and wondered if any of them had ever been touched – themselves or their loved ones – with this devastating disease? If I had only known then what I learned later, I would have been somewhat comforted. More than two million people in the United States suffer from schizophrenia. Even that fact is often hidden from the general public because many families don't want to admit to having a schizophrenic among them. It is a stigma most families would rather keep hidden in the closet. The famed Dr. E. Fuller Torrey called schizophrenics our "lepers" of this last century. Hopefully, new understanding of this brain disease will change this view.

I had been cheered by the thought of how much better John had been after two weeks at the beach. What had caused this improvement? Asking that question was in reality asking what causes the disease. And the answer is unknown.

About this time, John discovered that three of his local friends were looking for a fourth to share an apartment for their sophomore year at the University. In August, he loaded the station wagon once again with his things and headed to Richmond. He appeared happy, organized, and eager for a new school year.

He returned on Labor Day weekend for a family reunion. He seemed relaxed and in total control of his life. I continued to believe that John had been experiencing normal teenage and early adult feelings with the accompanying stress.

5 Full-blown Schizophrenia

AS I SAT on the park bench that day remembering the events that led up to the tragic announcement of John's illness, I realized how very wrong I had been to believe that all this was teenage stress. So much for my psychology skills! I wondered how John's birth father would have reacted to the news. He left home permanently for the West Coast when John was entering first grade and had died of cancer twelve years later. I know his death affected each of his five children in different ways. Some felt guilty, some felt anger, some were hurt and missed him greatly; all had to confront their father's death. Each one flew to California and took turns at his bedside.

At the beginning of John's second year in college, we talked on the phone at least once a week, usually when his bank account was empty.

One Sunday in October, I received a call from a physician in Richmond telling me that John had had an appendectomy. Later, when John came home to recuperate, he described the attack:

"I was at a concert in a crowd separated from my friends when this intense pain shot through my stomach. I thought I had been stabbed with a knife by the man standing next to me. I looked down and saw no blood. I went to the public phone and called the operator to order an ambulance to take me to the hospital."

John soon felt well enough to return to VCU. He seemed in good spirits. Just before Thanksgiving, I called to ask when he might be arriving home. He told me he had gone on a hunting trip and that his car had broken down. I told him to catch a ride and we'd worry about the car later. (What I didn't know was that he had gone hunting alone in the mountains near Charlottesville and had been stranded on a very cold night waiting for his car to be towed to Richmond.) He said he wanted to spend Thanksgiving with some of his Richmond friends.

I objected strenuously. I wanted him home for Thanksgiving Day but I also wanted to respect his decision. Once again, I compared him to his four siblings and remembered the many times that Duke University or the University of Virginia had played the surrogate Thanksgiving mother. However, I was just about to learn a bitter lesson: what had formerly been a successful way to raise children wasn't going to work anymore. The rules were changing faster than either John or I knew. Where we were headed, there were no rules – only chaos.

The coldness of that winter day was beginning to penetrate my heavy coat and I knew I had to start walking again to get warm. I also knew it would be months before I even had a hazy understanding of what schizophrenia was and what it was not.

My thoughts went back to the phone conversation I had with John the day after Thanksgiving, when he exhibited not only illogical thinking but "psychotic" symptoms. Only now in retrospect was I able to recognize those symptoms. He told me that he had written a check to the hospital for the appendectomy in the amount of $2,140. Surprised, I tried to make him understand that his checking account did not have that much money in it. He didn't seem to understand. I later found his checkbook with an imaginary $3,000 entered as a true deposit.

I called his roommate to get his viewpoint on John's behavior. Sandy was quite concerned. John was showing little interest in his classes, the very classes he seemed so enthusiastic about just a few weeks ago. He even told Sandy that he had seen his father alive and well and living in Richmond! I made immediate plans to drive to Richmond the next day to see John. But that very night, John was picked up by the police for trying to break into a motorcycle shop.

The next day, when JHS and I arrived at the Richmond Courthouse, we picked up a newspaper with the following account:

Another newspaper account quoted the museum director as saying, "We cannot speculate on the motives of somebody who would do something so irrational. I find it absolutely dastardly."

> AP – Richmond Nov. 28 – An 18th-century French painting missing from the Museum was turned over today to police by a local attorney ... there was no apparent damage to the oil painting. The painting's value was estimated by museum officials to be $250,000. The two-foot-square painting was reported missing Tuesday morning from its display position in the Museum's French gallery. The painting was acquired by the Museum in 1980. Richmond lawyer, John Smith, was watching television at home Tuesday about 10:30 P.M. when a former client "called and told him it [the painting] had come into his possession."... The lawyer said he would not reveal any identities to police ...
>
> According to Smith, his former client told him that the person who took the painting
> "ran in (to the museum) and ran out" with the painting ...
> Two key questions the police wanted to know were how security personnel responded to
> the alarm and how the thief was able to move through the museum without triggering other alarms, which include devices sensitive to movement and to heat.

When we saw John for the first time after these terrifying events, and the police brought him into the courtroom in handcuffs, he looked tired and blinked his eyes often as if he were trying to figure out why he was there. His eyes had an unnatural brightness, like someone with a high fever. He moved slowly to the front of the bench. The offense was read: "breaking and entering with intent to commit larceny; possession of burglary tools; and resisting arrest." Bond was set but the judge waived it and John was released to our custody. JHS (an attorney) explained to the judge that we were going to drive our son directly to George Washington University Hospital where he would be admitted for a psychiatric evaluation.

After hugging John, we found the cafeteria in the courthouse basement and chose a late breakfast. I looked at John wearing the knit Redskins cap with the bright orange tassel and wondered if he had been wearing it on the night of the museum burglary. Suppose somebody recognized him. I pulled it off his head and stuffed it in my purse. I could only deal with one burglary at a time.

John wanted to know why he was being taken straight to the hospital and not going home first. We answered that he had been released to our custody on the condition that we would get medical help for him. He seemed oblivious to the fact he might be sick. He told us that he had eaten some mushrooms on the recent hunting trip and that they must have been poisonous. I did not know what to think ... perhaps the mushrooms were hallucinogenic and caused that outrageous behavior. Since that was the only answer I had at the moment, I believed it. In a crisis like this, all of my coping skills were in high priority use and I had no time for quiet reflection. If a reasonable or unreasonable explanation appeared, I would accept it and question later. I needed the security of an answer, any answer.

We arrived at the hospital in the early afternoon and after six hours of grueling interviews, John was admitted. We met therapists, psychiatrists, psychologists, interns, students in medical school, and nurses, in single interviews and group interviews. At the very last interview, the admitting psychiatrist told John that he was psychotic and the he should be in the hospital for a complete psychiatric evaluation. John replied that he did not want to stay overnight and furthermore he didn't have a toothbrush and he needed to brush his teeth.

We urged him to sign himself into the hospital just for a short stay. He was not a minor at nineteen years. Just when our patience was beginning to wear out, the admitting psychiatrist announced to John that the hospital now had the responsibility to treat him and would be forced to recommend he stay there or be sent to a state hospital. He could have his choice. John agreed to sign in only if I would get him a toothbrush. I hurried through the hospital corridors to the gift shop, chuckling to myself about how my entire life at this moment revolved around finding a toothbrush. What great importance was suddenly attached to this everyday necessity! If the gift shop had been closed, I would gladly have paid a fortune for a toothbrush. I found one and John signed in voluntarily after meticulously cleaning his teeth.

We left him asleep on a bed in the psychiatric wing of the hospital, and were comforted by the thought that he was finally in the right place.

6 Hospital or Jail?

THE COMFORTING THOUGHT that John was in the right place did not last long. The severe strain of the last 24 hours continued but we were allowed no respite. The next day, I learned that John had signed an "AMA" – which meant he had signed himself out of the hospital "Against Medical Advice." Fortunately, from the time a patient signs an AMA, 72 hours must elapse before the patient is free to leave. The staff was not aware of the AMA until three or four hours before John was to leave. I was furious that I had not been informed.

Furthermore, I was no longer happy with the diagnosis of ingestion of hallucinogenic and poisonous mushrooms. Some poor fourth-year medical student caught the explosion of my anger. The student had mistaken me for a parent coping with life's vicissitudes who now had turned into a shrieking shrew. I attacked the entire hospital administration. Two results were achieved, both of which were positive. First, I arrived at the hospital in time to talk John into staying another couple of days. I told him that he needed to be tested for the poison from the mushrooms, and I explained that he might have to go to jail if he left because we had promised the judge that we would seek help for him.

It was not possible to reason with John in his psychotic state. I didn't even know what psychotic meant at the time and wondered why John was being so difficult. "Psychotic," I later learned, implies the loss-of-reality symptoms found both in schizophrenia and in manic-depressive illness, also known as bipolar disorder. The second positive result of my anger was the release of my feelings. The strain seemed less burdensome now and some calm was restored to me. Maybe we wouldn't discover instantly what was wrong with him. I was able to handle that. Had I known then what the next few days would bring, the new strength would have vanished immediately.

On John's fourth day in the hospital, a detective from Richmond came to question him about the theft of the painting. The hospital staff prevented the interview. That same day in Richmond, a grand jury returned two indictments charging John with burglary and grand larceny of the painting and issued an arrest warrant. We would have moved more quickly to find a lawyer if we had been aware of this action. Lowell Toms, a well-known criminal lawyer who specialized in defending the mentally impaired, was recommended to us. He agreed to take John's case and to try for a therapeutic solution.

I thought to myself, "Of course there will be a therapeutic solution, John obviously did not know what he was doing or he would not have voluntarily done such a "dastardly deed," using the words of the director of the Art Museum. Most people suffering with severe symptoms of schizophrenia plead guilty in court and become convicted felons, while people suffering with severe symptoms of other physical illnesses (Parkinson's, cancer, etc.) do not have to stand trial for their disease.

I had been with John on his sixth day in the hospital. When I left the building by the side door, armed police officers with the arrest warrant from Richmond entered the front door. John was arrested and handcuffed in the close psychiatric ward. This was so frightening to the other patients that the chief resident called a special "community meeting" at which he explained to the residents that John was wanted for some non-violent criminal charge. He quieted their fears and turned their anxiety into sympathy for John.

Meanwhile, I received a call from John's resident psychiatrist telling me the news. She reported that John was extremely nervous when he left with the officers and probably was in a state of shock.

My child, my son, poor John, handcuffed and hauled off to the D.C. jail just as if he were a savage murderer. John, the gentlest of all my children, the one who watched over baby birds learning to fly, the one who put itinerant grasshoppers back in the field, the one who made no secret of sharing a beautiful sunset with his mother – this was the hardened criminal being taken to jail? How could this sensitive soul ever be the same after an experience like this? What could be done now? I was hardly able to put the phone down and speak to JHS about this latest calamity. I felt totally helpless. All the good nurturing years of John's childhood and adolescence were now culminating in the torturing thought of his spending the night in a crowded cellblock.

JHS immediately called our lawyer, who in turn called the state police to learn the contents of the arrest warrant. The lead detective told Lowell Toms that the D.C. Police were only to arrest John if he tried to leave the hospital. Somehow, the teletype copy did not include those lines and the officers who arrested John were only following orders. My husband was able to obtain a hearing before a commissioner late in the afternoon. The question seemed to be whether John would spend the night in jail and be taken to Richmond in the morning by the state police or be released to our custody so we could drive him there for his court appearance in the morning.

I looked out the window at the darkening sky. Icy droplets of sleet were beginning to fall and coat the sidewalks and streets with a treacherous glitter. I hoped and prayed that this tender young man would be returned to us for the night.

John was arraigned before the Commissioner in Superior Court with JHS entering his appearance as the attorney of record. The Commissioner released John to JHS's supervisory custody with the understanding that he would take John to Richmond in the morning for his appearance in court.

There were no words to express my relief when I saw the two figures enter through our front door. The sleet and hail that had seemed so cold and merciless minutes before changed into a friendly winter evening. I hugged John, who looked tired. His eyes had that same unnatural brightness I'd seen before.

His yearning to be safe and secure was obvious. I wanted this weary stranger to be nurtured and loved by his family. Yet, I was afraid.

I did not trust his judgment. I did not know then how many months, even years, it would be before there would be any sort of trust between us. This game had no rules. There were none. In the past, our relationship had been based on a mutual faith. Once again, I would have to learn that what had been before no longer existed. I might as well have been a lonely visitor on the moon without knowledge or equipment to survive the trip. Even if I had known that John had suffered an acute schizophrenic break that made him feel torn apart from his own world because his mind had played tricks on him, I still would not have understood how to respond to him. How could I even guess at the hurt, humiliation, and hopelessness that kept recurring until he finally came apart? The coming apart, the psychotic break, has been described as an experience as terrifying as one's own death.

However, I wanted him back at that hospital as fast as possible. Instead, we ate the Chinese carry-out food that had been picked up on the way home. John sat in front of the fire for a long time, appearing to absorb its warmth as well as the warmth of being safe in his own home once again. Even I began to relax until he said, "Where is my gun?" Living in Virginia and hunting with family members was a normal event. My apprehension shifted into high gear.

Never dreaming that he would be home this evening, I had left the gun in his room. He decided to clean it. I tried not to appear concerned but I watched him until he finally finished with it. If I had been uneasy about his presence in the house that night, the fortune cookies that came with our carry-out made me laugh hysterically. My husband's fortune read:

"A special surprise is awaiting you at the end of this evening."

John's fortune read: "Get out in the social whirl as much as you can."

After a long night of reading and listening to every noise in the house, I was glad to see the dawn. We were soon on the road to Richmond. A thin glaze of ice covered the highway and at each bridge, cars were spinning into the abutments. If anyone deserved better conditions, we did. An accident would have compounded our problems beyond solution.

When the sun came through the clouds and the ice began to

disappear, I knew that things were going to get better. I looked at John. He was staring intently out the window and smiling his silly smile. He seemed to be so far removed from this time and place – the road to Richmond – that I wondered what road he was traveling. I was sure of one thing – that his road was a tortuous one, and a lonely one. I understood later that while John may have seemed out of touch with present reality, he was experiencing so many internal realities that he was overwhelmed and confused by them.

The inner agonies were requiring all of his time and attention and he could hardly even acknowledge the present circumstances. His facial expressions, first tormented, then smiling, were reflecting these internal terrors. He was struggling with a vacillating brain, a brain that was telling him that he would self-destruct if he acknowledged any of the chaos within.

The prosecutor met us as soon as we arrived at the courthouse. He was considerate and provided us with a private conference room. The lead detective escorted John through the booking procedure and we followed along part of the way. I watched John answer questions with the silly smile constantly on his face. I wondered how much he understood of the events taking place. The detective reported that John laughed so much while he was being fingerprinted that the clerk became angry.

How was the clerk expected to know that inappropriate emotions are a common symptom of schizophrenia, i.e., linking the wrong emotional response to a serious situation.

As we waited in the hall for John to finish the booking procedure, we overheard a news reporter in an adjoining room saying, "The museum thief will be identified soon; we think it was a student; hold the space." The reporter had no way of knowing we were right outside the door. My first cowardly reaction was to look for the nearest escape exit. I didn't want to be here. It was too painful. I wanted to run.

John's case was called and JHS once again stood up to speak to the bench. He described John's strange behavior and how we had taken him last week to the psychiatric unit, where he had been admitted for exhibiting behavior consistent with psychosis. The court gave John a date one month away to reappear and set a bond of $5,000.

Luckily, we were allowed to use our house as collateral if we promised to send the deed immediately to the court clerk.

We drove back to the hospital in Washington and John was readmitted. We were unprepared for the welcome the other patients gave him. They treated him as if he were a long-lost member of their family. The meeting that had been called to discuss his situation had turned into a powerful expression of their sympathy. The next day John's entire story appeared in the *Washington Post*:

I read this and suddenly felt the need for fresh air. The idea of John's problem being the breakfast fare of so many strangers made me break into a cold sweat. I walked out into the cool December morning to clear my head. I thought to myself, if I am really down at the bottom of the barrel, then I had been told there is no other place to go but up. I hoped this was going to be true. Visiting John later that day I was told that the evening before, he had been so agitated after the long day in court that he had to be confined to the "quiet room" and given a very strong dose of thorazine.

The quiet room, in reality, is a padded cell. John turned his attention to me only once to ask when he could come home. I explained to him that he needed to stay in the hospital until we found out about the mushrooms and that we had promised the court we would do this. I did not know then that in a few days, my argument for him to stay in the hospital could accelerate to the threat of either "go to jail or stay here." I left him sitting in his bathrobe and pajamas smoking a cigarette and staring at nothing.

STUDENT IS ARRESTED IN ART THEFT
WASHINGTON POST

A Virginia Commonwealth University student whose stepfather, a Washington lawyer, said had been

acting strangely since eating wild mushrooms on a recent hunting trip, has been charged with stealing a quarter-million-dollar painting from the Museum ... John deButts, 19, was charged with burglary and grand larceny in two sealed indictments Monday. He was arrested at a Washington hospital Wednesday and, under an arrangement worked out between his lawyer and the state police, was brought to the prosecutor's office yesterday morning by his family ... he was released after posting $5,000 ... the woman who helped recover the painting says the man who took it simply walked in the front door of the museum, went to the painting, put it under his arm and walked out. He presented it to her as a gift. She said he told her he got it at the art museum, but no one believed him. Later in the day, after some friends – art majors at the University – looked at the painting and decided it was valuable, she arranged to have it taken to the police ... The student was hospitalized in Washington after his arrest last week on attempted burglary charges unrelated to the museum theft. Police said the student was seen trying to enter a motorcycle dealership after midnight Thursday. Police were called to the scene by a citizen report, and when they arrived a man was trying to enter the front door of the building, in full view of passers-by. "He wasn't your normal B&E [breaking and entering] man," said a police officer. "It wasn't a smart deal." The general manager of the motorcycle shop said the burglary attempt was a "very amateur" effort. The would-be burglar tried to open the door with a credit card and stick and when that failed, by pounding on the lock. The door was never opened; instead police arrested the suspect and charged him with attempted breaking and entering, possession of burglary tools and resisting arrest. The lawyer for the defendant said the student had exhibited other signs of aberrant, though not criminal, behavior after the hunting trip ... "He is a very sick young man. I think it's clear that he needs intensive medical treatment. He simply was not in his right state of mind."

On January 7, a hearing is scheduled for attempted burglary charges and also, a Circuit Court Judge will set a trial date in the museum theft case ...

7 Mushrooms and Medication

EACH MORNING WHEN I awoke, I would relive the nightmares of the past ten days and wonder if my life would ever return to a normal state, such as worrying about what the weather was going to be like or what we were going to have for supper that evening. How I longed for those mundane thoughts.

Visiting the hospital was difficult with the sullen and uninterested John looking skeptically at us. This was no surprise to us because there usually was a pattern to his behavior during our visits. He would greet us warmly and give us one minute of his undivided attention. After that, he would withdraw into himself and we might as well have been conversing with a brick wall. I guess it was those inner agonies once again requiring his complete attention. If it was possible to pull an answer out of him, the words were always the same, "I'm tired." How could anyone perceive the extreme fatigue he was suffering in traveling that lonely road and fighting that vacillating brain, which was constantly deceiving him with inner tortures?

That same day, the doctor asked if we would agree to starting John on antipsychotic medicine. We were informed that the professional staff had ruled out marijuana, PCP, and mushrooms as causes of the psychosis. John was still sure that the mushrooms had caused the behavior and I had not tried to persuade him otherwise.

Several friends who had read the newspaper accounts called me to tell me of their encounters with poisonous mushrooms. "Watch him very carefully," I was advised: "mushrooms can be the cause of suicide in young people." I listened, but somehow even with my own uncertainties, I could not accept mushrooms as the prime cause of John's psychosis. To support my opinion, I consulted an expert at the National Institutes of Health, who told me that the mushroom poison would have been out of John's system 48 hours after he ingested them.

What really worried me at the moment was what would happen to John when the "life raft" of the mushroom theory was pulled away from him. Would he drown because he could not face an unaccountable inexplicable illness? If it had happened to me, I know I couldn't face my own irrational behavior. My sanity was based on a rational explanation of life, an ordered universe.

We agreed to start John on medication. What other alternative was there? Each of my visits was a duplicate of the one the day before. He would give me one minute of attention and then complain of boredom, lack of fresh air, and how people in general were picking on him. He would become enraged with me and ask me why I wanted him in the hospital. I always replied that I wanted him to get well. If he became too angry, I would say, "Well, then, go to jail!"

One day, I lost my temper and yelled back at him, "Do you think I want my son in a locked ward? Do you think I am happy over this? You must be crazy to think that..." – and then I realized what I had said.

Stelazine was the anti-psychotic drug prescribed for John. Within five days of 30 cc's administered daily, I was witness to a dramatic change for the better in John. He had responded to a behavior modification contract with his staff nurse simultaneously with starting the medicine. The contract simply reinforced appropriate behavior. Instead of the surly, angry and unkempt pajama-clad young man, a quieter, calmer, and neater John greeted me. He was quite excited that he had been moved from the locked hall to the unlocked hall, complete with private telephone.

The one piece of unhappy news was that the side effects of the medicine created a Parkinsonian foot shuffle for John and arms that did not move freely but hung stiffly at his side. While these side effects distressed me, his remarkable improvement was too good to be true. Another side effect which was not as immediately apparent was an insatiable desire for sleep. Before I even heard the word schizophrenia, the doctor in our family group session had mentioned another illness, "tardive dyskinesia." It was explained that this was a disease contracted from the powerful medicine Stelazine or other neuroleptics, in essence a side-effect. If John was monitored carefully and tested for signs of this crippling paralysis, he could be spared. The name caused me to wake from a deep sleep one night shouting, "it's tardive, it's tardive ... he's got it!"

The family group sessions occurred once a week with an intern as the therapist, since George Washington University Hospital was a teaching hospital.

At the fifth family session, we were informed of the tentative diagnosis of schizophreniform disorder. The therapist had explained previously that our presence showed John the family's love and support for him at this very difficult time. I wondered about that, because it always seemed that John was on the hot seat with his "loving and supporting" family gazing at him and thinking, "how in hell did you get into this mess?" He was required to answer questions at times and showed so much anger he just turned the whole group off.

After all, when the doctor and therapist were there, my husband and I, four siblings and a spouse – that was nine to one! If all nine of those people were sitting in a circle around me, staring at me and discussing my problems, I know I would retaliate either violently or by just passively ignoring them. Being a non-violent person, John usually chose the only path open to him, to turn his attention away from the nine "guidance counselors."

At the time of those early meetings, I thought that this was the only way a doctor and therapist could talk openly to the patient and the family at the same time and answer questions about the progress of the patient. What puzzled me was that the sessions usually turned into family therapy (our reactions to the situation) at John's expense. We could have met without him and satisfied our needs. I still have no clue as to whether those group meetings helped John at all and I am not sure they were beneficial to the family.

John was now enjoying fresh air walks with small groups of patients and staff members. He was informed that the more appropriately he behaved, the sooner he could earn an overnight pass to spend at home. He had many visitors during the holidays – friends from school, uncles and aunts and cousins, brothers, his sister, tiny niece, and brother-in-law, all somewhat awed by the strange circumstances of this illness but determined to show him their loyalty.

Sometimes John would walk so stiffly, shuffling his feet, holding his head and moving it from side to side with both hands, giving a cavernous yawn, sticking out his tongue, or staring at me with such an impenetrable gaze that I had to turn away in desperation. I almost wished for the former surly, angry, unkempt person. Yet, that person had not been making any progress toward getting well. If I questioned the medicine, I did not do so publicly. I was told that it is a popular pastime to attribute the symptoms of schizophrenia to drug effects. The truth is that those same symptoms existed fifty years before the drugs were introduced and the symptoms John was exhibiting were a direct consequence of the disease and its probable effects on his brain. The antipsychotic did CONTROL John's disabling symptoms, his thinking disorder, his auditory hallucinations, and his aggressive and bizarre behavior. The drug had proved itself effective for the symptoms that mattered most; if there were some strange smaller symptoms, then he would have to learn to live with them. I noticed that Stelazine did not have much effect on the schizophrenic symptoms of apathy, ambivalence, poverty of thought, and flattening of the emotions. John remained aloof, unable to sustain interest in reading more than a headline, had little or nothing to say, and seemed apathetic to any query.

When I was asked much later what Stelazine did physically for John's brain, I was able to understand that it blocks the transmission of dopamine in brain cells. All the neuroleptics essentially do the same things. There are hundreds of billions of cells in the brain called neurons that form electrochemical bridges transmitting impulses and making intrabrain connections. At these bridges, a chemical known as a neurotransmitter is released and travels to the next neuron. Of the more than thirty different kinds of neurotransmitters, one is known as dopamine. It is believed that during the psychotic phase of schizophrenia, there is an excess of dopamine transmission in the neurons in certain areas of the brain. Other neurotransmitters today are under investigation by schizophrenia researchers.

8 Day Care Program

AT THE SIXTH family group session at George Washington University Hospital, I was prepared to ask my hundreds of questions about schizophrenia. The family had been busy that week after recovering from the shock of learning that John had schizophreniform disorder. Medical bookshops had been visited, library references had been researched, and copies of articles from magazines and pages from psychology textbooks were duplicated and ready to hand out to the family members.

One of the first articles I read informed me that Charles Manson was psychotic and that the most common psychosis is known as schizophrenia. Psychosis means not in touch with reality, and most persons with psychosis might have schizophrenia. The article did <u>not</u> say that they also may have manic-depressive illness. The article <u>did</u> say that Manson probably had an antisocial personality disorder. I did not take any comfort in this knowledge.

So what was schizophrenia? I sat in the family group waiting to be enlightened by the therapist and the new doctor. Instead, we were asked about our reactions to the news and did we have any guilt feelings? My children, never at a loss for words, started to discuss their feelings. One felt bad for not speaking out against John's use of marijuana and perhaps that had contributed to schizophrenia. Others felt that John had been neglected over the years. The reason was that the three middle children had always been the dominant personalities, and Henry, the oldest, and John, the youngest, had never competed with them. Mary, Tom, and Read were the "squeaky wheels" who demanded all my time and attention and it was suggested that perhaps there had been no time for John.

The therapist then asked me if I felt any guilt for John's illness. At that moment, I never had considered the idea of blaming myself; it was foreign to me. I stated sharply and succinctly that there could be no connection between my actions and this disastrous illness. I realized I was calmly following my natural instincts and had I realized the full implication of that question, I would have been enraged. My background was that of a single parent divorced for twelve years with five children in the house, although the oldest one, Henry, was eighteen and "emancipated". "Emancipated," I learned, meant a son or daughter living at home who chose not to go to college and had a job instead. I also learned it meant a larger food bill and no child support for the "emancipated" child.

My only interest in life during those years was to oversee the development of these young people into responsible citizens armed with healthy egos and some education or skill so that they would be able to support themselves in society. I knew without a moment of hesitation that I had done all that was humanly possible to achieve this goal; this included hours and days and years of always being available to them to discuss or listen to whatever was bothering them. I also knew that someday I would be free of these restrictions, and while I would miss our close relationship I would cherish time of my own, and it would be a fair trade to give up one thing for another.

I was programmed by my own past in the forties and fifties when my role models demonstrated to me that self-sacrifice was the key to successful parenting. I thought if I sacrificed everything for my loved ones as the schools and churches had taught me that my children would benefit from my counsel and my example.

Just when I thought I had all the answers, I was forced to see what a genuine anachronism I was, trying to bridge the gap between complete self-sacrifice and full-time employment as a single working parent. If the "me-first" generation of the seventies had not arrived on schedule and relieved my guilt and anxiety about not being a full-time sacrificial mother, I would have burned out quickly. I made peace with myself about the quality of time spent with each young person (much extra time for the youngest), and it was also satisfying to know that I was not only preparing the food we ate but I was earning the money to buy the food.

The idea of my being to blame for John's illness was as foreign to me as the name and nature of his disease. I too wanted to place the blame somewhere, and as one friend who was commiserating with me said, "But, Polly, don't blame yourself, there is no way you could have spared John the trauma of divorce." Was this friend saying that had there been no divorce, John would not have schizophrenia? Are there facts that document a connection between divorce and schizophrenia? Does it mean the more traumatic the divorce, the greater the disease? At the time of the divorce, John was six years old and the disease arrived when he was age nineteen, after thirteen normal and happy years. No, I did not believe there was any connection.

In the sixth family group session, I was still waiting to be enlightened about this disease. Surely I would be handed a pamphlet outlining the early warning signs I should have noticed in John, or at least there would be some information on the treatment and outcome of schizophrenia. Was I witnessing an information desert? My entire knowledge of schizophrenia consisted of *The Three Faces of Eve* and the little I'd read about Charles Manson. I was being handed the myth induced by our culture that John was a split personality and a murderous maniac and, furthermore, I had caused it. If that myth was true, then I would join the silent millions who kept their secret in the closet. Nobody was going to know about my "leper" and accuse me of being the cause of it.

A week later, almost in answer to the information vacuum, Read brought a splendid book to us, *Surviving Schizophrenia – A Family Manual*, by E. Fuller Torrey, M.D. This book, published in 1983, became our everyday source of information, hope, guidance, and understanding. Without this treasury of knowledge and the unique perspective Dr. Torrey gave to schizophrenia, we would have floundered over the numerous decisions we had to make in regard to the best possible treatment for John. Since the role of caretaker fell to me alone in the days after John's release from the hospital, I followed Dr. Torrey's advice of using my own common sense and not ALWAYS trusting the experts. (Today, Dr. Torrey's manual for families , patients, and providers is in its Sixth Edition and totally up to date.)

At the next family meeting, we were told that John would be given a pass to come home for Sunday dinner. If the visit went well and he continued to show appropriate behavior, then we could expect him home permanently at the end of the month – and it would be eight weeks that he had lived in the hospital.

As far as understanding schizophrenia, the family had been reading Torrey's book and learning how little was known about this strange disease. We were unaware that we were following a well-worn path that could be called "state of acceptance" and that it was mandatory for us to accept the fact that John was sick before we could be allowed to learn what the symptoms, causes, and prognosis were going to be for him.

The home visits went well and John was to enter the Day Care Program the week before he was released in order to become accustomed to the hours and tasks. After being discharged, he would report back to the hospital five days a week. I felt comfortable with this arrangement. One day I talked to "the Professor," a fellow patient, and we both agreed on how difficult it was to be discharged from the hospital. A patient had to show more appropriate behavior than normal visitors from the outside. For example, during one of my more traumatic visits with John, and while he was brushing his teeth, I was so disturbed about having lost my wedding ring earlier in the day that I sat in the patients' lounge berating myself in a loud voice. When I finished my harangue, the ominous silence revealed staff and patients staring at me. They were not allowed to indulge themselves in this manner. I smiled weakly at them.

John was discharged from inpatient care on the 20th of January. I drove him to and from the hospital each day. Sometimes we had good days and sometimes we had bad days, each compensating for the other, and I was grateful for what we had. On bad days, John would tell me that he could not go to the program, he felt sick, he didn't have any energy, and he hated day care.

I was soon to learn that while John hated the day care program, it was not one-sided. Minimal cooperation and no interest other than to sleep was John's contribution to day care at this stage of his illness. We were told that he was deep into post-psychotic depression, a normal response to such a severe psychosis. When it was suggested to me that I should keep him up at night watching TV and not let him go to sleep before ten p.m., I rebelled. Even if during the day he found the nearest couch and spent as much time on it as possible, I would not keep him up at night. I decided if his brain had been sick, then it follows that, like any illness, the brain needed rest and healing at this time. Due to this philosophy, I was labeled in the medical reports as an "uncooperative parent."

The weekly family session centered around the fact that John was unable to plan his week's work at the Day Care Center. The report stated that he could not even copy a plan someone made for him. He bothered the other patients and annoyed the staff. He was acting more like a two- year-old than a twenty-year-old.

One morning on the way to the day program, John said, "People who rob museums are not well." I responded, "But you are going to get well. You have worked hard trying to get well. You are a hero overcoming tremendous odds. That is what heroes are all about ... doing the seemingly impossible tasks." All this was easy for me to say but did not change the loathing John seemed to have for the program.

"I don't want to live if I have to attend this day care program," he announced one morning on our way out the door. I explained to him that there was no other alternative at this time because of the pending court case and as long as he stayed with the hospital, he wouldn't be required to appear in court. I disliked his statement about not wanting to live and I immediately reread Dr. Torrey's opinions on whether schizophrenics were suicidal. As a group, Torrey wrote, schizophrenic patients are remarkably nonviolent. Timidity is characteristic of them far more than is aggression.

This comforted me immensely because one of the patients in the day care program had jumped off a bridge shortly after John had started the program. I made up my mind that John was not suicidal based on another incident. He complained to me one morning that he had been violently ill in the night, vomiting. Showing great fear, he told me that he almost choked to death on his vomit. He repeated several times in amazement, "I could have died."

At the next meeting of the family group, we discussed the medicine that John was taking and his Parkinsonian-like symptoms. He shuffled his feet, his arms hung in a gorilla-like manner, and his eyes were constantly blinking. Getting him up each morning to go to the day care program was a battle in itself. I tried to be cheerful, but the more cheerful I was, the angrier it made John. He didn't want to get up and he definitely did not want to go to the program.

Each afternoon, I tried to think of something John and I could do together before he went to bed after dinner. Sometimes we would go to a restaurant or visit a museum. He never showed any emotion over anything. He rarely smiled. I would babble on about trivial matters to be company for him, and occasionally he would make a comment. More often, he would bring up the subject of whether he would have to go to jail. Our afternoon outing always ended with this remark:

"I want to go home now and rest. I like to hide in my bed after day care. It's safe."

I was becoming more and more irritated with the family group meetings. The therapist who ran the meetings seemed to be more interested in the dynamics of a large family than in helping John. One session was devoted to the family language, terms the children had developed and used during their growing-up years, "inside" jokes actually. Also, if questions were not phrased properly, John would just repeat the answer the questioner wanted to hear. For example, "John, don't you think it is a good idea to have family sessions?" "Yes, I think it is a good idea to have family sessions."

A week later, I was called in by the day care program's staff director to meet with the entire staff to discuss John's behavior. They had several complaints. They felt that his unruly behavior was caused by a failure to take his medicine. I explained that I administered it and watched very closely to see that he indeed was swallowing it and not "cheeking" it. Nevertheless, I was told that from now on, he would have a liquid concentrate to put in his orange juice, and he need not know this.

"If I err," said his doctor, "I want to err on the side of medicine. It's classic, his not taking his medicine." I objected strenuously. I had been totally honest with John about his illness and the reasons for taking the medicine, and now I was supposed to sneak his medicine into his orange juice? How could he ever trust me again if I did that? I was going to win this round. However, John would not be allowed to continue the day care program unless his disruptive behavior ceased. It seemed to be a vicious circle to me. The more pressure that was put on him to stop the behaviors and join in the program, the more his behavior worsened. Stress made him sicker.

If I only knew how absolutely correct I was in believing that stress caused his illness to worsen. I was to learn within a week just how great a role stress played in his illness.

9 Stress

"It is as I suspected. The picture is that the examination by the legal people has caused a regression in John's illness." These were the words spoken by a doctor friend to me over the telephone in regard to John's recalcitrant behavior at the day care program. The pending visit of the state psychologist and psychiatrist to examine him was causing stress that was causing the illness to worsen. This was the vicious cycle.

In the meantime this excerpt from a Richmond newspaper appeared:

> ***STUDENT INCOMPETENT***
>
> Friday, Feb. 8 – A nineteen-year-old college student who was charged with stealing a painting valued at $250,000 from the Museum has been diagnosed as not mentally competent to stand trial.

And this, a few weeks later:

CITY ATTORNEY SEEKS TESTING OF STUDENT

The Richmond prosecutor has asked the Circuit Court to order a psychiatric evaluation of a man charged in December with the theft of a painting valued at $250,000 from the Museum.

A hearing has been scheduled Tuesday on a motion to have the student, 19, evaluated to determine whether he was capable of understanding charges against him and to assist in his defense.

In a report to the prosecutor, the doctors said that the student was suffering from a form of schizophrenia and was incompetent to stand trial.

The prosecutor said yesterday that he assumed the student was still a patient at the hospital. He said he was asking the court to determine whether this man could be examined by state psychiatrists.

The dates were set for John to be examined by the state psychiatrist and the state psychologist. His behavior was clearly a reaction to the pending visit and I had contributed to much of the stress by constantly reminding him that he had to stay in the day care program long enough to be tested.

During the time that I was called almost every day about John's bizarre behavior by the hospital's Day Care Center director, I wondered why these so-called experts decided John was my total responsibility. This continuing problem of his not fitting into the program caused me to question the program. Each day I would drive the car and pick him up. I would ask him how that day had gone and he would mumble, "Not so good." He was punished for resting and lying down, punished for making faces, punished for eating at an improper time, punished for lingering too long at a meal, punished for finishing his meal too soon, and on and on ... He was blamed for being uncooperative. Punishment was a series of points, and when he accumulated a certain number he was required to come two hours earlier to the program.

I was blamed for this uncooperative behavior. I was told I was too overprotective and that I interfered in his carefully prescribed treatment. The only interference I could see in the treatment was that I had to get up at five a.m. in order to get him to the program two hours early, a disastrous arrangement!

He had a hard time getting up, due to the effects of the psychotropic medicine … plus the fact that he didn't want to go.

JHS and I often discussed how much John was sleeping. The only guideline that made sense came from our friend and occasional handyman, Albert, who was unable to read and knew nothing about psychosis except that John had a "head" problem of some sort. Albert said, "When de brain is broke, it need rest like any other part of the body when it broke." Plain common sense: of course, John's brain needed rest!

I referred to Torrey's book, which usually answered my questions. Withdrawal can be used as a means of coping with the internal chaos, I learned. Resting and reclining and sleeping are means of withdrawal.

A typical morning conversation with John would go like this:

"Good morning, John."

"Why do I have to go to day care?"

"To get the charges in Richmond dropped. The court thinks you are there. They want to send their own state doctors to examine you. When that's done, we can think of other possibilities."

"I think I am going to throw up."

"If you throw up this nice breakfast I have cooked for you, I will be angry."

"I don't want you to be angry. I deserve day care because I took the painting."

"No, you don't. You were ill – you didn't know what you were doing when you took the painting. I'm so proud of the way you have handled your illness. I couldn't do as well … Your mind played tricks on you … That's what happened, and it must have been terrifying – frightening. You are the HERO … someone who has to deal with a chemical imbalance, a real disaster. People write books about heroes … That's why I'm planning to write about you."

Though I tried my best to make John feel better and reduce his stress by praising him, I think what he heard was just so many empty words. However, I wasn't joking about writing a book about him. I was determined to tell the silent millions (those who kept their "lepers" in the closet) the story of John's illness and his fight with it.

One evening, we had a conversation in the kitchen. John was just sitting down to eat a very hot pot pie and I was at the sink. We had just laughed over a past remark by Russell, Mary's husband. He had been trying without any success to comfort his crying baby, who was teething, and he had looked up at us woefully from the rocking chair and said, "That's why they call them babies." At this moment, John was pounding his fists loudly on the table, singing over and over, "Hot, hot, burn, burn, hot, hot, burn, burn," and all of a sudden I lost it. My patience was gone and I burst out without thinking:

"And that's why they call it schizophrenia!"

John looked at me quietly and said, "That's mean."

I had done it. I had said the name of the illness for the first time. I couldn't believe I had said it to him. I know I wasn't reducing the stress on John by naming his disease, but then I felt the stress, too. What if the state psychiatrist said he wasn't sick? Maybe he would go to prison after all.

Another conversation took place a day or two before John was to see the state psychiatrist. He was in bed when I came downstairs to his bedroom to say goodnight.

"I know you must be tired tonight," I said.

"I want to bite somebody."

"No."

"Yes, I will."

"Why?"

"I have to."

"No. Good night; see you in the morning."

"Stroke my head."

"OK." And I stroked his forehead softly as I have done so often. "You're going to get well."

"No, not ever."

"Yes, you're doing great. It takes a while. You're overtired. When you do all that funny stuff, I think you're overtired. What are you thinking about?"

"I can't tell what's in my head."

"Just rest and relax."

At this stage of his illness, John often asked me to stroke his forehead, which caused the same reaction in him as if he had taken a tranquilizer. He would relax and become quite calm. The experience of being touched, research shows, plays a critical role in the growth of the body as well as that of the mind. Touch is said to release brain chemicals promoting physical growth, according to these studies done with infants. For the first time, researchers are determining that touch, the neurochemical effect of skin-to-skin contact is a form of communication so critical that its absence retards growth in infants. If this is true, the stroking of John's forehead released certain chemicals in his brain and helped him regulate his response to stress.

JHS and John were constantly conversing with each other by bantering back and forth in verse, each giving one line. This conversation took place on the way to day care. I recorded it, remembering what Dr. Torrey had written about how rhyming in short couplets was a characteristic activity of the illness.

"Old Tom Noddy, All big body."

"Hot toddy."

"All big body."

"Mayor Mayor has lots of hair."

"Hot toddy."

"All big body."

"Like many of the upper class,"

"He liked the sound of broken glass."

"The King of France"

"Wet his pants."

"Hubba, hubba,"

"Goodrich rubbah."

"Day care, I swear."

"Does day care suck?"

"It sucks; it bites."

"Does it bite the big one?"

"It bites the Big GREEN WAZOO!"

"Does it bite every hour all day long?"

"Harcourt, have you been drinking again? Harcourt Fenton Mudd sat in a great big tub."

As we got closer to the hospital, John started making funny noises with his throat. It seemed that the minute he felt any stress, his symptoms returned. He would start beating the air with his hands. The hospital always seemed to invite this stressful behavior.

Later that same morning, a call from the hospital came at eleven o'clock. "We cannot persuade John to get up; he insists on resting." Small wonder, I thought, he had risen at 6 A.M. in order to get there early to be punished for sleeping the day before.

The stress was so great that the director decided to hospitalize John. She did not consult me. When I arrived at the hospital in response to her telephone call, it was too late. There was a sign on the sixth floor between the two elevators that said, "Do not allow John to leave this floor." How primitive that was. Why was he singled out for this treatment? The director's explanation was that John had been playing with some knitting needles and did not put them down when he was asked to do so. She was fearful he might be suicidal.

When I objected to the hospital stay, the director threatened to order John's visit with the state psychiatrist canceled unless I agreed. The threat worked. I backed off because I did not want to jeopardize the examination. I felt I had been blackmailed. After the examination, I knew what I had to do and that was to remove a very unhappy person from this bad situation. Yes, John was sick, but he was also very unhappy.

I guess I understood more about stress at our favorite Chinese restaurant two nights before the psychiatric examination. The three of us, JHS, John and I were just seated at a table when the weird behavior began with a loud burp, hands on his head as if he was straightening it, and then fluttering his hands as if playing an imaginary piano. There was a blonde girl sitting at a table across from him. He never took his eyes away from her and she was visibly getting uncomfortable. I tried to distract him from doing this and talked about the Shrimp with Lobster Sauce the waiter was putting in front of him. I saw that his eyes were closed and his lips were trembling.

Without any warning he opened his mouth and vomit flew across the table like a projectile! Luckily, no one was in the line of fire. If we hadn't been so surprised by this event, we might have been more upset. We knew we had to get him home quickly but how do you walk out of a restaurant full of diners with any dignity after an episode like that? We extended our apologies, paid the bill and left. We never returned. Later, at home, when John was feeling better, I asked him, "Well how is old 'projectile' doing?" He actually smiled.

The next night before the psychiatrist's visit, I was giving him a dose of medicine when he asked me, "Day care tomorrow?"

"Yes." I said.

"I feel violent. I'd like to cut somebody."

While my thoughts were racing, I said, thinking of Torrey's advice.

"It's good you can express your feelings. You're going to get well ... Rest now."

A few minutes later, when I was outside his door, he called: "Come here!"

"What?"

"I threw up!"

He was lying on his back in his bed and there was vomit all over the bed and the floor.

"Wow," I said. "Maybe the oysters you had were too rich..."

"Where'd they get the money?" he asked.

"That is funny. Pure corn." I replied.

"I feel rotten. Maybe a cold?"

"Take an antihistamine."

"How many do I have to take to O.D. (overdose)?"

"That's not funny," I said.

"Why should I take my regular medicine?"

"Trust me, you need it."

"What would happen if I stopped?"

"You'd end up in the hospital again. You can decrease the dosage – but not stop it."

"How will I ever get out of the program?"

"The only way out of this program is to stop all this weird behavior and they will let you go."

The day of the testing finally arrived and the summary of the results is as follows:

Summary: This 20-year-old white male is charged with theft of a valuable painting from a museum and attempted break-in of a motorcycle shop. This occurred about five months ago. It is believed that he is competent to plead and stand trial and was competent at the time of the alleged crime or crimes, though the alleged crimes may be considered the product of a mental illness, either psychogenic but more probably drug induced."

(signed) by Licensed Clinical Psychologist
April 1985

According to this evaluation of John five months after the psychotic break, there's nothing much wrong with him. He is competent to stand trial; he was competent at the time of the crimes; and the reason for the crimes was probably because he had smoked too much pot. Evidently, the report by the George Washington University Hospital doctors which stated that he was not in possession of his faculties at the time of the theft was ignored.

At least the examination was over. What a relief – for me as well as John. I thought back to an interview JHS and I had had with a state psychiatrist. We asked him so many question because we felt that he was sympathetic to us, and he was the first person who took the time to explain the disease to us.

"The man's mind has virtually been wiped out... his personhood no longer exists. Like a broken leg, you can't walk on it; slowly, it will get better. John copes as well as he can; he goes in and out of the shadows. If he can cope and there is no excess stress, he may avoid another break. He needs pedestrian speed ... and you must rebuild his ego. Positive reinforcement. You look puzzled. How can you do this? You start with small questions like, 'John, where do you think I should add grass seed to the front lawn?' He will give you an answer. Take the answer and build on it. You say, 'that is a really good idea. You are right, that is the area that needs it. A really wise decision.' If you do this once a day, messages will be sent to the brain telling him that he knows something and that he is a worthwhile person. Gradually, enough of these messages will build his ego again. Perhaps in five years, you will see an improvement."

Five years! I was not able to believe that. I could not let go of hope that he would get well. I was not at the stage of his illness where I could accept it. Like the stages of mourning a death, I was still in the stage of early grief, unable to admit the inevitable. I believed in a complete recovery.

With the examination finally over, I was determined to find some other program for John. Before I even had a chance to look for one, I was informed that John's behavior had been so uncooperative that he was suspended from the day care program. I felt totally adrift. I had wanted to change him slowly and with a great deal of preparation. My security blanket had been jerked out from under me. I needed to investigate other programs while John was still under a doctor's care.

I knew John had enough medicine to last for a week. I was so relieved when I heard that the doctor at the hospital would continue to prescribe until a new program could be located. The hospital did care after all...

I started my search for a new program with a Dr. Elizabeth Farrell, a therapist who ran an alternative psychosocial program for psychiatrically recovering individuals. The description read, "For the recovering person who wants to make friends, do useful work, and become more self-sufficient." This was ideal – except that John was not ready for this program. I sadly realized this after a long telephone conversation with Dr. Farrell.

She was the first medical person who expressed sympathy for my situation. I wept as she told me she understood what a difficult situation I was in. She said, "What you need is an M.D. with a biological concept of the disease – the frame of reference is biological; support therapy is helpful, but not psychotherapy. My program meets the emotional need of day-to-day therapy, never focusing backward."

"I am like a crew boss or team leader to about six young people. We do volunteer work. We give a task to the ill person, and the completion of the task makes the person able to think of him or herself as being worthwhile. It builds their confidence. The usual day care centers are very depressing. The work I do is designed to make these young people act as normal as possible. If they think of themselves as 'schizos,' well, that is bad."

"If you need references for doctors, you should call the Northern Virginia – Alliance for Mental Illness (NV-AMI). They know the good doctors and the bad ones. Don't pay any more money for this illness; connect with the state mental health facilities. Don't forget to apply for his Social Security disability..."

She had given me enough advice to keep me busy for months. I immediately called the center and asked for an interview with the director of the day care program. (I was so happy there was no cost involved.) I made an appointment at the Social Security center and I called the local NV-AMI. Mrs. Jack of the local group soon returned my call and told me the story of her son. Thirteen years ago, he had had an episode and four years later he had to be hospitalized again. She told me that the local group known as Pathways was a support group for families of chronically mentally ill patients. I told her I didn't know about the "chronic" part but I'd certainly like to hear about the experiences of others. (At this stage I was not accepting the fact that John could be chronically ill.)

Looking back, I am sure that Mrs. Jack had heard these words from many parents who were new to the illness and could not accept the "chronic" side. She said tactfully, "Well you just never know about these younger ones and what will happen."

10

A Wedding and a Memo

WITHOUT MUCH WARNING, the weather turned warm. It was spring and there was going to be a wedding for John's brother Tom. The long bleak days of winter were over; the sun was making its formal debut with all the pomp and glory of soft breezes and bright flowers. The weather change was as welcome as the change from dwelling on John's problems to making plans for the wedding.

Planning the rehearsal dinner for fifty was a full-time job. Sending the invitations, renting chairs, tables, linens, polishing silver, cleaning the house, ordering flowers, and arranging the seating was a wonderful distraction. We all wondered if John would be able to handle the stress of being a member of the wedding party.

"He's my brother and he's going to be in my wedding," stated Tom with finality. No one wanted to argue with Tom and no one did. Meanwhile, in a placid manner, John went for his tuxedo fittings with the seven other groomsmen.

Four days before the wedding, a friend came by in the evening to take John out to a movie. I was happy for him to have the invitation but told the friend to make it an early evening. It was early all right: at 6 A.M., the car pulled into the driveway with John looking pale and sick. He went right to bed and barely ten minutes later, I heard him being violently ill in the bathroom.

Aside from this pre-wedding illness, John performed beautifully at the wedding. Standing at the altar, he remained motionless, blending in with the other groomsmen. The bride was glowing, the groom smiling; on the surface, there was tranquility. How many in those church pews knew of the rough waters underneath? The turmoil that preceded this day? I was relieved to have John's public appearance accomplished. When one considers the tremendous effort this required of him, he seems almost heroic. When one considers the tremendous risk this required of both sets of parents, they should also be considered heroic. Anything could have happened – but it didn't. In my nightmares, I had covered every catastrophe I believed possible.

The days that followed the wedding were all good. In a strange sense, I felt as if John had rejoined the human race. Being part of the wedding and wearing the identical clothes as the other young men seemed to have boosted his ego. He had been accepted as an authentic member of the wedding party and not some freak who could not control his own mind and thoughts. He was no longer monosyllabic. He spoke in sentences. He began to think of other things he had previously enjoyed. He wanted to rebuild his tape collection. He spoke of getting his car fixed so he could start driving. For the very first time since the illness, he seemed relaxed. We had come such a long way from that depressing dark day in January when I was washing some of John's clothes and a flattened empty pack of cigarettes had fallen out of his shirt pocket. I had picked it up and held it in my hand, saying to myself sadly, "This is the only interest he has these days and before he had had so many. His whole life was ahead of him."

All these improvements in John did not seem to last very long. About a month later, I picked John up from the Mental Health Center that he had started attending regularly. His face had been painted to resemble a clown's. I looked at him and wondered if this was a tangible expression of how tired he must be of himself, his life, and this terrible disease. I knew I was sick to death of the disease. What I didn't know was the extent of my loathing of the illness. I soon learned this.

After mowing the lawn one hot day, I came into the kitchen to get a drink of water. John started patting my head as I leaned over the sink to splash water on my face. He pulled the kerchief off my head. I replaced it. He pulled it off again. This happened once more, and the months of my aggravation came tumbling forward and I lost control.

It was as if I had been saving up all my emotions for this very moment.

"Don't DO THAT! I'm sick of you. You won't get up in the morning, and you sleep late, especially when I need help with the lawn. You burp in my face; you won't brush your hair, or take a shower." And my lowest blow came when I said, "Even the therapist says you should be on a schedule, and you should help with jobs around the house. You live here, too, and you don't do anything to help." Ganging up on him with the therapist was inexcusable.

He just stood looking at me for a long time, then quietly turned and left the kitchen. My tears flowed as I realized what a giant step backward I had just taken. All the building up of the ego I had worked on ... shattered by a few razor-sharp words. How could I have indulged my emotion?

Later that day, I apologized to him for my outburst and made an effort to let him know that it was the illness that made me so angry, not him. He then, for the first time, tried to explain his actions to me.

"Sometimes I want to talk to you, I want to speak to you, but I don't know how. If I repeat words over and over, I know I'll get your attention. Maybe pulling your scarf off your head over and over again was like repeating words."

Another conversation the next day demonstrated that he had heard my accusations and was slowly responding to them.

"When I yawn in your face and burp, it's because you are telling me something I already know. You say take four pills. I know that. I get frustrated with you." What is he telling me? His inappropriate behavior is caused by frustration, which is the same thing as stress?

I developed a memo (based on *A Parent's Creed*) as if written to me from John to help prevent any further outbursts.

MEMO TO PARENTS
FROM
A SCHIZOPHRENIC SON

[words which will never be spoken]

1. **Don't spoil me. I know quite well that I ought not to have all that I ask for ...**

2. I'm only testing you.
3. Don't be afraid to be firm with me. I PREFER IT. It makes me feel more secure. I will never tell you this. I said FIRM, not mean or angry. I need the limits you set for me.
4. Don't let me keep bad habits. I have to rely on you to detect them. I may not be able to do anything about them but if you mention them, I will remember. I am trying very hard to live with my disease and adapt myself to the world at the same time.
5. Don't make me feel that my mistakes are sins. I know it is my illness that you are angry with, not me. Please explain this to me; it helps me understand why you are often short-tempered with me. Remember, I have a difficult time accepting my own illness.
6. Don't be too upset if I say "I hate you." It isn't you I hate but your power over me. I am dependent on you to survive and I HATE that.
7. Comfort me but don't take too much notice of my small ailments. Sometimes I need the attention they provide for me.
8. Don't forget that I can't explain myself as well as I should like. This is why I'm not always very accurate although I try to be.
9. You may ask me a question but don't rush me for an answer. It takes a while for me to process a thought. I cannot answer two questions at the same time.
10. Don't put me off when I ask questions about my illness. If you put me off, you will find that I will stop asking and lose the trust I have in you. And I don't want to know everything about my illness all at once I only want to know answers to my specific questions.
11. Don't tell me my fears are silly. They are terribly real and you can do much to reassure me if you try to understand them. You don't have to comment.
12. Please understand that while this disease has allowed me to retain some of my former motor skills, like driving the car and some sports skills, I am helplessly regressed at other

times and remind you of an annoying, irritating ten-year-old kid. I do this most often when I am relaxed and with my family. I cannot explain this behavior or other facets of this illness. Sometimes I think the illness is gone, only to have it reappear when I least expect it.

13. Don't forget that I cannot thrive without lots of understanding love, but I will never be able to tell you that. Most of my thinking capacities have been devastated and I often feel I am virtually a wasteland.

11

A Therapeutic Solution?

OUR LAWYER INFORMED us that John would have to be hospitalized for three weeks in Harrisonburg, Virginia, where one of the most respected authorities on schizophrenia, Dr. Showalter, resided. With Dr. Showalter's careful observation of John's illness, the lawyer was gambling that the court would regard this valued third opinion, which could lead to a dismissal of all charges. A therapeutic solution.

When John learned of the pending hospital visit, he demonstrated many forms of stress. The first one occurred right after he had been told.

"Don't leave me there."

"I'm not leaving you, trust me."

"I feel weird."

"That's because of the hospital visit."

"Am I going to the D.C. jail?"

"No, no, just to the hospital."

"I'm going to eat some mushrooms."

"That is not funny."

"Old Tom Noddy."

"All big body."

He started clinking the spoon he held against the glass he was holding. He also reverted to holding his head in his hands as if he was trying to straighten it. I had not seen that behavior since the hospital in December. I certainly remembered what stress does to a person in this condition.

It was during these three weeks that I realized I wanted to write a personal firsthand account of John's illness. I wanted to tell the story of the disease to the caring people who, like me, knew nothing about schizophrenia until it struck. I wanted the people who asked with concern, "Does he assume different personalities at different times?" to understand this disease. I wanted to look at the disease in retrospect and learn from the experience. I wanted to tell the many others who suffer with loved ones that they are not alone.

Three weeks later, John returned home from his hospitalization. Our lawyer called to give us his interpretation of Dr. Showalter's report and told us that the trial date has been set. The report contained good news and bad news. The bad news was that John would always need some sheltering and might never be fully independent. In five years, John might be able to hold a low stress part-time job. And if this was the bad news, how could there be any good news?

The good news was that there was no question that John had been psychotic at the time of the museum theft and the attempted breaking and entering at the cycle shop. This fact would make our case very strong in court. But the stress of a trial could well cause more permanent damage to John. And the last thing we wanted to do was run the risk of a jury or a judge deciding that a jail sentence might teach John to stay away from psychedelic mushrooms. The potential jurors are people whose knowledge of schizophrenia equaled mine at the beginning of John's illness. If the prosecutor told me that drugs caused the disease, I would have believed it. If he had told me that John's parents were responsible for the disease, I would have believed it. If he had told me that John's illness was caused by childhood trauma, I would have believed it. I am thankful now that I know that schizophrenia is NOT caused by any of those reasons. Yet, jurors would not know what I knew and might decide on a jail sentence. We would not go to trial under any circumstances.

So what were the alternatives to trial?

Waive the jury and depend on the court;

Admit guilt, plea bargain with no punishment. (John would be a convicted felon and would have to secure a full pardon from the governor of the state at a later date to restore his civil rights.)

If this trial was stressful for me, I could imagine what it was doing to John. Dr. Showalter's words gave me great comfort: "The law entangles the medical profession but if we have enough information on our side we will get a therapeutic solution."

For John, there was no comfort, only symptoms of stress due to the upcoming trial. He was uncooperative at the center, seemed disoriented, was violently ill several times, and resorted to the rhyming couplets. He told me he was frightened of the trial and thought he might have another psychotic break.

We both knew that stress was making him sick. To support that belief, an article appeared in the daily newspaper. Dr. Leonard Stein, medical director of Dane County Mental Health Services in Wisconsin, spoke at a conference, "State of the Art: Caring for Persons with Chronic Mental Illness." He stated that "residual impairments" remain after a psychosis subsides in a mentally ill person, and that these persons are very vulnerable to stress.

At this same conference, Dr. Gerald Hogarty, schizophrenic research director at Western Psychiatric Institute and Clinic at the University of Pittsburgh School of Medicine, said that patients who have schizophrenia manage their lives best when they're helped by a combination of low-dose drug therapy and family and social support. A safe place to live and a low dose of drugs help buy time between psychotic breakdowns. He said drugs alone aren't enough to keep patients from having relapses. Those patients who live with relatives who are critical of them tend to relapse at a higher rate than those who live in more accepting supportive homes. In Dr. Hogarty's research, no schizophrenic patient had relapses for a year in families where there was a reduction in criticism and expectations of the patient.

What a revelation: If I followed Dr. Hogarty's advice I could keep John from having another psychotic break indefinitely. That very day, I resolved to throw out any expectations I had about John's life style, and while I would encourage him, I would not criticize him. If he slept until noon, I would say, "I'm glad you had a good rest. You must have needed it." JHS and I had been doing some of this, trying to build back his ego, but now we would take it further.

And, miraculously, in July, the prosecutor announced that all charges against John had been dropped. We had our therapeutic solution.

12 The Long Road Back

ON JANUARY 27, 1986, the Challenger exploded. Everyone knows the rest of the story. I never felt the nation's sadness over this accident because I was grieving over John. One explosion shook the world; the other one occurred quietly in his mind. He did not have a second psychotic break but was on the verge of one when we hospitalized him.

The events that led up to this day could have been foreseen by Dr. Hogarty. We had followed only half of his advice; we had supplied the safe and supportive environment but no medication. Six months earlier, John had announced to me that his doctor at the center had ordered him to immediately stop the Stelazine. I was shocked.

"We suspect that John is showing early signs of Tardive Dyskinesia and he can no longer tolerate his medicine. We just hope that it is in the early stages." So my original dream was not unwarranted; he could have Tardive.

Where was I supposed to go from here? Try to see how John got along without any medicine? I vowed to be flexible and do this. Maybe I could be the mother of one of the one-third of schizophrenics who get completely well.

Life was easier without having to remember John's doses of medicine each day. Normal living was returning and I increased my hours of consultant work. However, I watched him very carefully. His emotions were raw and unprotected. He seemed to get angry very easily.

He started working in a rehab program and drove his car by himself to his job. Sometimes he complained about the type of work he was doing, cleaning vacant apartments. Within two months' time, he seemed less confused and much happier with himself. He could only work three or four days a week. A cold, a cough, a sore throat, and an upset stomach were the reasons. These were the classic symptoms of stress. The job was stressful.

However, I wanted to believe that John was far better off without any medication. I was not recognizing the symptoms of stress he was exhibiting.

One day, John quit his rehab job, saying, "I'm worth more than $1.28 per hour." We agreed. He looked for construction jobs and worked a few days. It was obvious that he was confused, had disconnected thoughts, and extreme paranoia. When I described these symptoms to a social worker, she told me to get him on medicine as quickly as possible. It is a common occurrence for a schizophrenic to become psychotic after six months without medication.

Just the weekend before, John had complained of the dangerous small animals that often came into his bedroom at night and frightened him. Finally, he agreed to go with us to the center to be evaluated, but when we got there he refused to take any medication.

We agreed to commit him to a hospital for 48 hours' observation. Dr. Rao, a soft-spoken pleasant woman, had suggested this only as a last resort in order to get him on medicine. By hospitalizing him, his condition would be stabilized. Since he would not go willingly to the hospital, the police were called to take him there in handcuffs (on the advice of Dr. Rao).

The next day, I visited John in a stark white room, the size of a closet. There was no chair, no table, no bed, no picture; it was indeed a cell. John, wrapped in a sheet, was sitting on the floor with knees pulled up against his chest. His body posture told of the anguish he must be experiencing. He was humiliated and embarrassed by the treatment. He believed he was being punished. The seclusion had robbed him of what little self-esteem he possessed. His similarity to a wild animal caught and caged, frantic to be free, was an overwhelming statement.

"If you had just told me, I would have taken medicine. You let me down." I could not tell him that we had asked him to take the medicine.

John was provided with a lawyer and a hearing was scheduled for the next morning. The lawyer advised John to agree to take the medication and he could be released. I had no argument with this.

But once John was home, he again refused to take his medicine. He said he was crippled by the side effects. And he was. His neck was stiff, his feet shuffled, and his eyesight was blurred. While we waited for an intake appointment at the center, he became more and more angry over the previous hospitalization. His anger turned inward and became frustration, most of which was directed solely at me. I began to understand the evils of this disease. Its vicious nature followed a tortuous cyclical path. Six months without medication brought on a prepsychotic condition, which carried its own natural factors. As John became more and more psychotic, he felt the need for medication less and less. But the less medication, the greater the psychosis.

Strange events began to occur as John remained untreated during the Spring months. One day, I drove home to find the driveway to the house blocked by a beautiful spruce tree that had been chopped down. John had decided there were too many trees in our yard. Three more trees were felled before I successfully pulled the chain off the saw.

Early one morning, John drove in with a large dead deer. He had been hunting all night in the country with his bow and arrow and his dog, Ralph. Ralph, a timid house dog, was visibly shaken at having to share the back seat of the VW with a dead deer. I was visibly shaken when I learned John was going to dress the deer himself on the backyard patio. According to the previously established pattern of John's behavior, I would be called on to finish halfway through the dressing.

I had never cut up anything larger than a chicken. I prepared for my duties by getting the hose, the wheelbarrow and many garbage bags. John began to feel weary and asked if I would help. He disappeared to his room and I cleaned up. The blood flowed, the deer hairs were sticky, and I prayed that the garbage truck brigade would not be suspicious about the warm body in the bag. Cleaning myself in order to go to work that morning was a challenge. I sympathized with Lady Macbeth.

John had a habit of driving his car into the driveway and then sitting in it with the motor running for at least 15 minutes. When my daughter asked me one day why he did this, I replied in a matter-of-fact tone, "He has told me that he sits and waits for small animals to clear the driveway." Mary, listening to the nonchalant, vaguely comical tone of my voice, said she knew at that stage I had finally accepted John's illness.

My earlier inquiry into the possibility of obtaining Social Security disability payments for John resulted in an interview during this period. I didn't bother with my usual efforts of asking John to comb his hair or change his clothes. This was one time that appearing ill might pay off. He passed this test with flying colors. When asked what he did for a living, I almost choked trying to conceal my amusement.

"I hunt small animals."

"In this populated county?"

"Yes."

"And what do you do all day?"

"I drive around looking for work."

"Have you worked steadily?"

"Oh, yes, hunting small animals."

"Do you do this regularly?"

"Yes, that's the way I get my food."

Suddenly, the interview was over.

In John's room, the dried squirrel skins seemed to increase in number and we guessed this was part of his idea of foraging for food.

It was at this point that we were ready to re-hospitalize him. He had traveled the same cyclical path, six months without medicine generating the pre-psychotic condition.

But this time, there was a difference. When we presented the alternatives to him, either take the medication or enter the hospital, he immediately agreed to go on medication. We made an emergency appointment with Dr. Rao. She started him on Melleril which has fewer side effects than Stelazine and Thorazine.

I did not know at the time that John would be stabilized on this medicine for many years.

13

Just Getting Along

THE FAMILY RELAXED. Melleril was the answer. While not over-medicated on this drug, John was able to contact several construction bosses and obtain jobs with them. Fortunately, the days that John did not show up for work did not cause him to be fired.

In 1987, my husband and I moved with John into Washington, D.C. JHS and I both had grown up in the District and we loved the city. Our jobs were there: JHS' practice of law and my job in the Administrative Offices of the D.C. Public Schools. It made sense to live there. I liked the anonymity of the neighborhood we chose, it was a relief to start over in a new environment after 23 years in the same house. I did not know anyone except the neighbor who shared the common wall of our "new" one- hundred-year-old duplex. The age of this dwelling gave me a feeling of stability and I pictured earlier owners sitting comfortably on the front porch watching the horses and carriages going by on the road. I learned that the 200 year old oak trees surrounding the area were part of a farm owned by Henry Foxall. He also owned the nearby Columbia Foundry which made cannons for the government. As the British were invading and burning the city in 1814 he made a promise that if his Foundry survived the invasion he would build a church. The well-known Foundry Methodist church is the result today.

John improved so much on Melleril over these years under the care of Dr. Rao that it was hard not to have some hope for complete recovery. (I should have paid more attention to Dr. Torrey's words of wisdom, that the diagnosis of a person at a younger age with a gradual onset of the disease is more likely to have a poorer outcome than one with a quick onset at an older age). I did remember the careful diagnosis of Dr. Showalter, "an undifferentiated type of schizophrenic disorder." So, reluctantly, I accepted that for the present and near future John was "chronically mentally ill." The local support group, formerly known as Pathways to Independence, NV-NAMI, played a leading role in my understanding. Several of these meetings with other families describing their son or daughter or husband demonstrated to me that John was very normal for a schizophrenic and I had better count my blessings that he was not any worse.

A sample of the comments from the meetings:

> *"Jim lives in a room by himself. If I mention "work" he gets very upset. Each time he gets a job after two weeks he goes to pieces."*
>
> *"The only way we got Gene to move out of the house into an apartment was to go with him. Eventually he liked it and we moved back into our house."*
>
> *"My daughter will not admit she has a problem. She does not come home any more except to get money."*
>
> *"The police had to come and handcuff Fred because he lost his temper and started threatening the neighbors."*
>
> *"When my son stops eating and sleeping I can see the signs of approaching psychotic behavior. We increase the medicine."*

I also learned from the group how I had originally reacted to John's illness. A mother enthusiastically told about her son's remarkable recovery from an episode. He had a full-time job and was gladly taking his medicine. She was asked how long he had been sick and when she replied only six months you could feel the gloomy response of the other families though nothing was said. Looks were exchanged. For the first time I graduated from newcomer to old timer because I understood the sadness. The sadness was how much more this poor mother would have to experience before she could graduate as I had, to accepting the illness. The very same response had been given by me when I first joined the group and knew for sure that John was going to get well. Maybe all the others would continue to have a sick relative but not me! My John was different. He would get well.

We worked on rebuilding John's damaged ego as the State Psychiatrist had indicated we should. For example, any accomplishment, no matter how minor, we complimented him for it. It could have been his neatly trimmed beard, or the nice fresh shirt he was wearing, or how happy he makes his dog Ralph by feeding him regularly. John's basic needs are the same as yours or mine, friendship, love, a secure place to live, job, etc. Living in the separate apartment we had built for him in the basement gave John the option to dictate the amount of time he wished to spend with us. Each evening, emerging from his apartment and smiling warmly at us, he would extend his hand in greeting and ask the same question, "How was your day?" When we thought of how his day must have been with all the outrageous mind-baffling difficulties he had to overcome to reach this common evening milepost, we felt he deserved a cheering squad! John was so well stabilized he took two weeks each summer at Wrightsville Beach with the entire family. John and his loyal dog Ralph would drive south in the truck he used for Handyman purposes. In the Spring of 1994 John flew to Hawaii to visit his brother, Henry, for three and a half months. He evidently benefitted from this trip because he returned looking very fit and settled. When he saw Dr. Rao, she indicated that she was reducing his medicine.

However, John was extremely lonely. One day I found a full size air filled plastic doll in his bed. He tried different ways to meet girls, through singles and church groups, but nothing materialized until one day he stopped to help a person whose car was stranded on the side of the road. Janette was her name and after she was sure that John was not the Boston Strangler, they started dating. Within a few months John had a new roommate in the apartment, Janette!

14

Bright Future

JANETTE SEEMED TO be just the right medicine for John. She was a small, cheerful and pretty person clearly in control of her own life. Her American Indian heritage allowed her to be totally accepting of John's illness. In fact, right after they met, John showed her the Richmond newspaper clippings all about him. (I thought, he could have waited a day or so........but he wanted it all out in the open..... and he was right). Janette believed that John had been touched by "divine intervention" and therefore was a "chosen" one. I rolled these terms around in my head thinking to myself how much better they sounded than the words regularly used by doctors and the newspapers, "chronically mentally ill." I could be pretty happy with the "chosen" one!

When Thanksgiving came that year Janette cooked a tasty turkey and gave the scraps to Ralph. These would be the last scraps Ralph would ever have because he had developed cancer and we sadly had to say goodbye to our dearest dog. John and I held Ralph's paws while he quietly went to sleep. I knew this was upsetting for John to lose his longtime, faithful companion but with Janette in the apartment there was little time for sadness. She commanded and John gladly obeyed. The apartment expanded into the basement with racks built for the new occupant's clothing. I wondered how long these very tight quarters would be comfortable.

In December 1994, the family celebrated John's 30th birthday with lobsters and champagne. Ten years had gone by since that terrible 20th birthday with John in the hospital and the doctors making the awful declaration of "schizophreniform disorder." How that name had haunted me over and over again, the memory of those Day Care sessions when John was punished for sleeping, for not participating in the activities and for acting weird due to the stress caused by the pending trial in Richmond. Now John seemed settled and relaxed with Janette. (Could anyone envision where John would be on his 40th Birthday?)

By spring, a townhouse in Manassas with so much space was too appealing for the couple in the tiny apartment and they signed a year's lease. Oh, Janette, how you have changed my life! It was strange for me not to be in charge but I realized I had the same feelings when my four other children had left home after college. I had learned mainly to keep my mouth shut and only give advice upon specific request. Even if I felt a wrong road was being taken – it was to my advantage to keep quiet. Sometimes, I could say in a breezy manner, "Have you thought of this….?" And, then stop. In order for those fledgling adults to continue to grow and learn they had to make their own decisions. In this case, with Janette in charge it was hardly necessary. She arranged the move, she helped John search for a job, and she encouraged him to apply at a hardware store. When he was hired as a Sales Associate he was thrilled. And, at about the same time, Dr. Rao declared that John need not take any more Melleril as he had been on minimal doses for the past two years. Hurray! What a bright future for John! And what a huge relief for me! After all these years I could relax at last. I did not have to think about John's pills, his pains, his stress and his loneliness.

However, during that first year of working at the hardware store and living with Janette there was some stress for John. One day he inadvertently set off the spray nozzles in the ceiling at the store. Luckily, he was forgiven due to some faulty plumbing and kept his job. I did observe that Janette had an unusual amount of energy and often it appeared that John was not able to keep up with her. She loved to meet friends after work adding to her very long commute to and from the city each day. None of this seemed to bother either of them until the day Janette lost her job and circumstances changed rapidly. Due to the loss of income they decided to vacate the townhouse and move back to the basement apartment. John made some nice improvements to it but it did not change the size – it was still a tiny apartment.

I knew that all was not well between the two of them, having no job was extremely difficult for Janette and John's job made him too tired to take her out at the end of the day. Further, she fantasized that perhaps John was not faithful to her. There were many arguments downstairs. All of this ended when Janette discovered that she had to have an operation and would need to recover for four weeks in the apartment. I know this was not a pleasant time for her, normally a person on the go - with unlimited energy! I would come home from work each day and find her occasionally on the deck in the sunshine deeply depressed. I could tell that she was trying to make decisions about the rest of her life and that she was going to move on. Probably the best decision. After she was well recovered she left. John was sorry but greatly relieved. They continue to be close friends with each other to this day.

The following year brought more changes to our lives. It was time for me to think about retirement. Retire? I wondered what that word meant. Do nothing? I had heard many stories about people who retired and worked harder at volunteer jobs than they ever had in their career jobs. As I gazed out my window on Pennsylvania Avenue I saw large buses pulling up in front of the Old Post Office building and men and women all carrying umbrellas climbing aboard each coach. When I asked about these people I was told that they were City Tour Guides. How interesting, I thought. Perhaps I could try this? I did, and after 3 months of study I secured a license to be a Washington D.C. Professional Tour Guide. What a challenge! My first fear was that a tourist would ask a question which I could not answer but gradually I understood that it was possible to say "back to you on that"! Tour companies began to hire me and I was launched! I realized, too, that Tour Guides are very bossy and talkative people (which they have to be) and I wasn't sure I even liked them. Gradually, over time, I discovered that I had become one of them, "bossy and talkative," and somewhat of a "know-it-all."

The most rewarding part of this job was that I did not think about John during the day, I was so involved every minute, planning, working with the Tour Leaders, giving directions to the Coach Operator, and, talking on and off the coach about the monuments and memorials. I told myself either you become a Tour Guide or you can stay home and wrestle with John's problems. The choice was easy, guide or die!

At this same time, JHS was facing a cancer operation and I was invited to carry the Olympic Torch downtown. The cancer operation was successful and "Granny" ran with the Torch. I am sure the reason I was selected was because of my age – over 65. Not that Granny was a freak but at least much older than all the young athletes involved. Meanwhile, John was busy with his job and proud of his record at work. For me this was the time I felt there might be a future for John and looking back with 20/20 vision the book should have ended here on this happy note.

15 Downward Slide

THE FIRST WARNING signs signifying that all was not well with John slowly began to appear. He complained of back pain, stomach pain, and headaches. He visited several different doctors, even some pain management seminars. All the tests proved nothing. I was beginning to fear that this process sounded all too familiar to me. Was John searching for answers once again? Was each trip to the doctor for this inexplicable pain a mute cry for help? Was he once again experiencing a last-ditch effort to maintain some self-respect while facing enormous odds of overwhelming defeat? Did he know something was very wrong? John's regular doctor finally referred him to a Psychiatrist and stated that John showed signs of anxiety, panic disorder and depression. Of course, John immediately replied that he did not need to see a Psychiatrist! All he wanted was some pain medicine. There was nothing wrong with him. Why couldn't the doctor understand this?

About this time, I became familiar with the term "Anosognosia." Once again I was facing an unknown medical term similar to when I first confronted the word "Schizophrenia." But there was a huge difference! This term gave me hope. It is a symptom of his illness. It is a deficit in his brain functioning caused by damage to specific parts of the brain. John is severely unaware of his own illness. He admits he had Schizophrenia when he was in college and that caused him to go into the museum and take the painting but that is past history today. He believes his pain, delusions, and hallucinations are real and not part of his illness. He is not in denial about his illness, he is simply unaware of it.

In spite of all the torment caused by his aches and pains, he faithfully appeared at his job each day for work. He was answering the phones and acting as cashier and I could tell that he was encountering a great deal of stress. But one day he met Alice, a thin, friendly woman. I was so happy for him thinking that Alice would be another Janette and help calm him down. For about six months John appeared pleased and elated. He even brought her to the beach that summer. She was a talkative and enjoyable person although at times she seemed tense and anxious. But anybody having to deal with our large and boisterous family could be excused for being anxious. As I was pursuing other interests, so glad not to be the "on-call" caretaker, John was trying to continue his old lifestyle and be a companion for Alice. He loved hunting wild turkey and deer and could afford to do this due to his job. One cold December day when he was out by himself the scope of his gun recoiled into his forehead. It evidently was a tremendous blow. He claimed he was unconscious on the ground for a period of time. He recalled, "There was a lot of blood, I'm amazed that I lived. I don't know how long I lay on the ground. Finally, I got up and drove myself to the hospital."

Now, there was even more reason for John to try to medicate himself, he had severe head pain. He was looking everywhere for relief. Alice was also in pain. John had told us earlier that when he met her she had been using special drugs to numb her arthritis. Evidently, the "special" drugs were street drugs and so together John and Alice sought help for their pain on the streets of Washington.

In early 2001 two catastrophic events occurred within the same week which would shape the next ten years of John's life. I thought to myself, what a good thing it is that the future is totally unknown. I've always wondered to myself about this as I contemplate my own death at some unspecified moment. Am I so afraid of this unawareness? I think not. William Hazlitt's words come to mind and invariably cheer me up. He wrote,

"... life has a beginning as well as an end. There was a time when you were not: that gives us no concern. Why then should it trouble us that a time will come when we shall cease to be? To die is only to be as we were before we were born."

The first of these two disastrous events happened on a Wednesday when John was fired from his job. After five years of working there he had lately developed habits of not reporting on time and, worse, falling asleep on the job. (I attributed this to the street drugs that he had recently been taking for pain). How could anybody work and be under the influence of narcotics?

The second event on Friday involved Alice. John had recently moved back to his apartment after several months of living with her. She had told him that they would not be seeing each other anymore. Whether she had a foreboding as to her future and whether she planned it or not, John learned she had died from an overdose of a street drug. He had not yet understood why they wouldn't be seeing each other when this shocking news caused him such grief. He began to question reality. He visited her grave often to reassure himself that she was really dead. He tried to offer his sympathy to the family but they were angry with him because they believed he had encouraged her use of street drugs.

Delusions, hallucinations, and even an apparition threatened John. He called the Police about the guy next door who he believed had murdered some people and maybe even Alice. When Officer Eliot appeared at our door he understood and said to us, "John thinks it's real." Knowing that John needed medicine we rushed to get an appointment for him. Of course, the doctor advised us that if he is not dangerous to others or to himself it is very difficult to have the Police pick him up. We knew this from fourteen years ago when Dr. Rao had called the police to hospitalize John. How could I have forgotton? So, now what?

John had other plans. He would take his car and drive away for a day or two. Sometimes he would go out in the country to visit his hunting buddy Ray, but most of the time he was self-medicating with street drugs in D.C, percoset and oxycontin at first. His behavior was so eratic that JHS and I looked for a drug rehab facility and found Warwick Manor.

16

Dual Diagnosis: One Step Forward and Two Steps Backward

ON JOHN'S VISIT to Warwick Manor, he wrote the following account of his use of drugs.

"In early 2000, I met a girl who I really liked. We soon lived together at her place. I had a very bad knee, a displaced knee cap. I had acquired some Demoral pills. I found out that she wanted to have some and before long we ran out. She told me she had terminal cancer. She wanted heroin and I got some for her. We used it together and had great fun. I decided that since she had cancer that she could have whatever she wanted. In 2001, I lost my job and days later she died. That really destroyed me. I began using heavily. It made me feel like old times.

"But three days ago I decided I was really destroying myself. I told my mother about the problem, I told her that I wanted to come to Warwick Manor."

This explains the next couple of years. Evidently, several rehabs were not enough. As I was busy religiously counting John's pills each day to be sure that he was taking them for Schizophrenia he was busy self-medicating himself with street drugs. It took me quite awhile to understand what was going on. Of course I didn't want to believe this and so I attributed many drug-induced actions to Schizophrenia. Looking back it is easier to understand why he had such sudden mood changes.

For example:

"How did you sleep?" I ask one morning.

"How did you sleep?" he replies in a sarcastic tone. Normally, whatever 'normal' might be, John was never a mean person. This was not his nature.

"And, don't ask where I'm going ." Then, he rushes out the door, is gone for about an hour, returns and is in a very good mood.

"So you are going to lunch?" he smiles. "If you see Sue, tell her hello for me. I may do some work on my car today."

And this:

"We must see Dr. Brannigan this morning," I said.

"You go see her. I'm not," John retorts angrily.

"Stop it. She's your Doctor. I'm not going to argue. Just go," I said.

"I would rather go live on the street than go through this," and John angrily slams the door as he leaves the house. And I continue to do my usual simple-minded counting of his pills.

Upon returning a few hours later John is quite mellow. He states, "I am sorry if I was mean , I think I had better clean up the apartment today."

Each week it seemed there would be an incident. Some nights there would be a loud knocking on the front door after midnight around two or three in the morning. It would be John needing money to pay the cab driver who had driven him home. He often said he was in Georgetown and did not want to walk home in the dark. There had been a night he came home with a black eye. Another night he came home with a missing tooth. One night the Crown Victoria station wagon which John had been using disappeared. John reported it stolen. Magically, it reappeared the next day with several new dents in it.

The next week, John's truck was missing. He claimed he had lent it to "Shorty." Why he would lend it I had no idea but later I understood it was part of a payment for street drugs. The truck was more difficult to find because John did not have a complete address as to its location. Finally the truck turned up in a public housing project in Northeast Washington. As we drove over to pick it up I wondered how long these incidents would occur. I believed my name was changing from the "Care-giver" to the "Enabler." Money was liberally flowing from John to these debtors like "Shorty." John could not hold on to any cash. If he had a one-day construction job the money was gone before he even arrived home. I should not have been surprised but I was unable to comprehend how clever a drug addict had to be to support a habit. This was all new to me and I was still daily counting his pills thinking each day about his random improvement.

The station wagon was missing again one morning. The police located it and we were able to pick it up where it had been impounded. But by this time the car had suffered so much damage (smashed in on one side with no gas gauge or speedometer), I wasn't sure I even wanted it anymore. My husband and I joked that when we heard the words several different mornings, "Car's missing!" We both hoped it was true even though our outward words were, "Oh, oh, so sorry."

Something funny did occur as I was giving a tour of the city on a 50 - passenger motor coach. We were stopped by an abandoned car at the Tidal Basin on our way to the Jefferson Memorial. As I was saying, "Our third President only wanted three accomplishments written on his tombstone, and he was most proud of the third one, the establishment of the University of Virginia..." I stopped to catch my breath when I realized the car blocking us was my own Crown Victoria. There it was in all its glory, both doors wide open sitting in the middle of the road.

As the Park Police pushed it to the side of the road, I stated indignantly, "How inconsiderate of the owner." The tour group never knew the car blocking us belonged to me. It turned out John had lent the wagon again to a drug dealer and when it ran out of gas the driver just ran away. A few weeks later the wagon disappeared forever except for coming back to haunt us with parking tickets from other cities.

John had been ordered by the Doctor to have a series of tests, Catscan , MRI and blood work to see if there was a reason why his head hurt. The tests all came up negative except for one. We had to laugh at that one because after all of these expensive tests, John's cholesterol proved to be off the charts. He had eaten bacon and eggs just before the test.

Could things get any worse I asked myself? Yes, money was starting to disappear from my purse. First, small bills, then big bills. My husband John was missing $100.00 in quarters from his briefcase. And this was only the beginning.

A typical evening conversation went like this:

"I need to borrow $400," John says.

"What for?" I say.

"I owe money."

"What do you owe the money for? You need to tell the truth. What exactly are you on?"

"I owe for the $25 percoset pills I bought for pain last week. This will be the last time I borrow money. I am quitting."

"If you can do that, we will back you big time."

Another conversation:

"I owe $375 more. I have to pay because it gets higher by the hour," says John.

"What are we going to do? I can't keep giving you money," I say.

"This is the last of the debt. There will be no more after this. But I have to pay this because they will come after me if I don't."

I look at him and say, "If this really is the last of all the money owed, then I will help you."

I cannot even remember the number of times these conversations occurred. I was as bad as he was, thinking each time would be the last. "The Enabler" was most certainly my name. However, there would be a period of a couple of months in between requests and I would quietly rejoice. Maybe I was right and this was the end. I did not know that the end was not even in sight yet.

I had to have a hip replacement one summer. The best nurse I had was John. At the hospital John came and sat very quietly for hours just to be there in case I needed him. At home he took responsibility for my needs and fixed many of my meals. As I began to get well he began to incur debts again and I was the "Enabler" once more.

One evening John announced that he had met a girl who started coming often to the apartment. By now I was very suspicious of new "friends." And, this time I was totally right. This "friend" stole checks from John and cashed many of them before she was caught and had to serve jail time. She also took my old Electrolux Vacuum Cleaner which really bothered me.

17

A Life Out of Control

I KNEW THIS was true – John's life was out of control. Looking for help, JHS and I went back to our dear Dr. Torrey, who recommended an associate, a Dr. Knable, who immediately started John on Geodon. This was an intermediate measure but not an answer.

The missing money continued. We knew John was trying to give up these street drugs but his valiant efforts were not enough. He claimed if he did not pay the dealers they would kill him. Over and over again he wrote me notes, "This is the last time I will ask for Polly to pay my awful drug debts. If I ever take drugs again I will leave this house, never to return. (signed) John"

Life at our house was almost untenable until Woodley House, a D.C. Public Health Agency, let us know that a transitional home for recovering drug users was available. As I drove John to this Valenti House where he could stay for a year I began feeling as though I had really failed him. Had I done enough? After I dropped him there I looked back at him standing there so forlorn with his suitcase in hand and my tears flowed.

But as I recalled the morning before, I knew this was a better solution, at least, for us. I had awakened at 6 am, and JHS, a much earlier riser, came into the bedroom and said, "I cannot find the car." Panic grips me; oh, no, John has stolen the Camry and probably given it to drug dealers … our only car.

JHS says he went to look for his wallet which he thought he might have left in the car but the car was not there. I could not believe it, I think, I am not going to have a fit though I felt like screaming… so, JHS has to call a cab to go to court and luckily, I do not have any tours this morning. Just as JHS is getting into his cab, the Camry arrives with John in it. He looks very sheepish. He explains, "I took the car. I wanted and needed to be with a woman. I am so very lonely. I got caught in traffic… and did not get back in time."

I am speechless. So, he caused us the greatest stress… and now he is apologizing.

He says, "I will never do this again. I have embarrassed myself and I am sorry for you." I listen, I think… it is not drugs… it is SEX. That is good news; no drugs involved. I had assumed this was all about going to buy drugs.

I did ask him naively, "what is she like? The woman?"

He replied, "She is older but nice, I was just so lonely." By then I knew I had better not ask anything else. Later my husband and I laughed when I told him my thoughts of how relieved I was that John had not used any drugs but that it was all about sex. I can understand sex but not drugs. However, I was to learn that I had been totally wrong about this incident and drugs had been involved as well as sex.

Although John was living elsewhere, he came each day to our house. I had hired him to help clean out the attic and the basement. I wanted to see him and find out how he was coping in his new circumstances. He had a large room he shared with a roommate. He attended house briefings, some counseling sessions and AA Meetings. I felt sorry for him, perhaps I had not done all I could have…he still seems so possessed by these voices, these messages. He describes them as many radio commentators talking at the same time, he catches part of what they are saying, a lot does not make sense. He quotes them, "What shall we do with him? He is worthless, it doesn't matter. Kill HIM. Too much trouble to even do that."

Now that John was settled at Valenti House, my husband and I decided to go to Barcelona, Spain and visit another son. We planned to be gone for about a week. What a change it was to be in Barcelona. Two days before we were to return home, a message came through to us at our hotel. It was from John.

"I broke into your house. I stole $700. I want to apologize for this." Did I hear right? He is apologizing to us for breaking into our house and stealing money? (JHS' law office was in our home and he kept sums of money there.)

WHAT TO DO? WHAT NOT TO DO?

When we arrived home we found a chagrined John humiliated by his own actions. We explained to him that we would have to call the police if he broke into our house again. Nevertheless, we changed all the locks.

Another trip to visit our daughter's art show in New York City occurred in December on the weekend of John's 40th birthday. We had celebrated his birthday earlier since we were going out of town. The irony of what happened that day never fails to amaze me. John spent most of his birthday in the D.C. jail. He had tried to buy street drugs from an undercover police detective, was arrested and incarcerated until his case was called. His brother Tom spoke for him and he was released.

The consequences of this day turned out to be one of the best things that ever happened to John. He had to go for drug testing twice a week for a year. D.C.'s laws really helped us out this time; if he stayed clean for a year all charges would be expunged. I was ecstatic! He had resisted Drug Recovery Programs in the past but this seemed to be another way out. He realized the seriousness of the situation and faithfully showed up for his appointments. If he failed on a drug test the year would be extended or there was a possibility of jail time. This scared him.

After a year in Valenti House, it was time for John to find other housing. Since John has always loved Virginia and his brothers lived in Arlington, we looked for rooms to rent there. A basement room with shared facilities in Ballston was chosen. He was also introduced to the Arlington County Department of Human Services where he received his meds, Abilify, at this time. John liked being independent. But with that independence came the responsibility of taking his meds which did not seem to be happening.

I would question him at least once or twice a day, "Did you take the pills this morning?"

He would reply, "Yeah, I think so."

What kind of answer was that? But I held my tongue, "Could you check the number and see?"

"Yeah, I'll do it later."

As a result, after 10 months, John called me one morning on my cell phone while I was giving a tour at Mount Vernon and said that al Qaeda had planted a bomb in his building.

"Planted a bomb!" I repeated loudly while several tourists listened.

They gasped and asked what should we do? I said, "Don't worry, this is just a television series my son watches!"

With that, my tourists seemed mollified and I calmly explained to them how farmers in colonial times branded their animals on their ears. Today, Congress uses earmarks to arrange for special funds to be used for projects in their own states.

As we walked past the "haha" walls surrounding the Mount Vernon lawn, the phone rang again and this time I told John to come to our house later and we would talk about the bomb. John was agitated and he said he thought he ought to report it now.

"Please don't," I again urged him.

So much for my advice. The next thing I knew, the police had called and said that John was being taken to the Arlington hospital because he had told the people living in his building to evacuate immediately. He was admitted to the psychiatric ward.

Of course, we heard from John's landlord that John was no longer welcome in his rented room. That figured. We looked elsewhere and found another small room to rent with shared facilities. No questions asked.

Although John was better having been on his meds regularly during and after the hospitalization, I still wondered what the future would bring as far as regular use of his meds. And, should we change dosage?

The voices continued to plague John. Sometimes he would call and say, "I'm going to the hospital, I don't know what else to do. The voices are driving me crazy, I'm so mixed up, I can't sleep. Every thought I have, ten voices jump in to discuss it." I would urge him to come and stay at our house. And, often, he stayed a few nights taking

Seroquel (a newly prescribed drug for him).

"How many people live in D.C.?" John asked.

"About 590,000," I reply.

"Then there are about 300 al-Qaeda agents here, and they steal your thoughts," he replied.

"Who?" I ask.

"I can't tell you again, they'd be angry," he said.

"They mess with your brain?" I ask.

"Exactly!" John replied. Occasionally, I am admonished for questioning him.

"Stop! You have asked me enough how I am. I cannot stand a question every minute. I won't be O.K. if you continue."

John did admit to us one evening, "I'm taking too much Seroquel, maybe I'm addicted. I need to be off the stuff for awhile. I lost the bottle and can't renew it anyway." He sounded so rational and sane. Then he looked closely at me.

"I believe you have Schizophrenia, why don't you try some Seroquel?" Hearing that remark, I was ready for the whole bottle.

18

Quiet Desperation Or The Bottom of the Barrel

ONE MORNING WHEN John arrived at the house for work, he told me, "It takes all my energy to fight these voices. Every few seconds I hear them saying things like 'get him', 'kill him', 'he's gonna die'. I get so tired of listening to them. I think I am like a wild animal in the forest. I run and run but there is no place to hide from them."

This conversation makes me think that the meds are not working - or was he not taking them? I decided to write to his psychiatrist and describe what was going on. I had never met his doctor because I thought my presence might inhibit John from opening up and talking more freely about his problems.

MEMO TO DR. BARRERA 03/05/07

Re: John deButts

John's meds do not seem to be working for him. He is hearing voices constantly. At least once a month he feels he must stay at our house (in D.C.) where he feels safe from al Qaeda who chase him on the street. The Seroquel does give him a sleeping aid from the voices. John's past history with Meds shows that Meloril with Cogentin was the drug which originally worked well. He was on it from 1987 to 1995 when his Psychiatrist discharged him. He worked at a large hardware store for 5 years. In 2001, his girlfriend died. She had overdosed on street drugs. At the same time John was fired from his job. He had suffered a head injury and also started taking street drugs for the pain (Percoset and Cocaine). Dual Diagnosis. He went to Warwick House (a Drug Rehab facility) twice for drug treatment, and for a year he lived at Valenti House in D.C. continuing his drug rehab. He had been living with us but when he started taking money to buy drugs he could no longer live at home. During this time he was alternately on Geodon, Risperdal, most recently, Abilify and Seroquel. John was arrested in December 2004, on his 40th birthday for buying street drugs. After successfully reporting for urine tests for a year all charges were erased. He moved to a house in Ballston but when in 2006 he reported that a bomb was going to go off he was hospitalized. Since then he is with us everyday (does odd jobs around the house), calls us daily to tell us that people are after him and the police should be notified. I hope you and John can figure out a way to get rid of the voices or least get them under control. They are so very real to him.

Thank you for your interest and help.
Polly deButts

I did not know at this time that all signs were pointing to another hospitalization.

Early one spring morning as I was emptying the trash, I noticed the empty carton of TIRAMISU. The box had been purchased the day before as it was one of John's favorite desserts. There were eight servings of this high calorie delightful Italian "pick-me-up" in the box, so-called because Italian women, traditionally, mixed the left-over expresso with a touch of liqueur and mascarpone for a mid-day energetic lift. All of the contents had been consumed by John in one evening. No wonder he was gaining weight. And, we did read that one of the side effects of Seroquel is a gigantic appetite.

That same morning John came to me with a paper he had been working on. He explained that he had figured out what had happened to him and wrote it down so that I would understand.

John writes:

"From a feeling of being really scared, long ago I created a body double (not flesh and blood) and placed it in Afghanistan. I was drawn into this like a vacuum due to the Soviet invasion of this country. Then I forgot about it. Years went by....

By November 2001, I had figured out what had happened. It came to me in bits and pieces. I understood by making this double of myself I had become entangled with the government's main frame computer. Here's the story:

A few years after 9/11, I was at a friend's house for dinner when a senior government official was bothering me mentally about my drug use.

"Stop using drugs!" he repeated over and over again. He was relentless.

Finally I responded, 'Go to Hell,' I replied using the same type of communication the way I had received it!

I suddenly felt a wireless electrode go into my chest and while shaking violently I fell on the floor. I figured that it was high voltage from a satellite shocking me through that same official's use of the main frame computer.

My friends were very concerned about me. Should they call 911? Since it only lasted a few seconds, I assured them I would be fine.

This was just one incident.

Over the years, thousands of electrodes have been put in my body. From what I could tell there were several people doing this to me with instructions typed out telling the computer what to do. It then projected an invisible image and uses anyone's voice. I have spent hours listening to these different voices. The electrodes have a low voltage and begin to hurt the longer they are in my body. I find this extremely painful. One was in my body and created a lump on my back (and is still there).

The computer projection of this invisible image which is not seen but talks to me becomes a great burden by following me everywhere, 24 hours a day. I knew the wrong people were in control of the computer! For a person like me who already has schizophrenia, this added inconvenience makes it 100 times worse.

With as much strength as I can muster, (you see me clenching my fist and getting red in the face) I reduce the power of the body double which drains my energy. This can help."

As the longer days of summer arrived, our family began looking forward to the annual gathering at Wrightsville Beach, the North Carolina barrier island. All 25 of us, siblings and cousins enjoy each other's company in this relaxed atmosphere and as the Matriarch of the bunch, it's a treat for me to see the grandchildren grow so beautifully into their unique personalities each year.

Before the first signs of trouble with John occur, I rise before dawn to sit on the deck facing the ocean. I drink in the soft morning light so fresh and clean like a new beginning and watch the tall dune grass in serious attendance, nodding delicately to one another, waiting for the sun.

Trouble starts in the afternoon when John tells me that in the sound directly behind the cottage there are Russian submarines. He has called 911 to report them. The U.S. Coast Guard returns the call and two local police appear, one a former Marine. They were extremely kind.

The next day, John walked up the street and stood for 20 minutes staring at a cottage while the owner was sitting on the porch. He made the owner so nervous that the police were notified. Officer Robert Davis arrives and reports to me about John's activities and he seems to understand that John is hallucinating about the al Qaeda terrorists living in that cottage. He says,

"If they are there, I'll find them and report back to you, John."

Meanwhile, some members of the family, unaccustomed to

such bizarre behavior, were getting extremely nervous and wanted John hospitalized immediately here in North Carolina. In fact, they threatened to do it if I would not. They needed a better understanding of the situation. By patiently explaining the characteristics of the disease, including how scary the name "schizophrenia" is yet how non-violent are the majority of people with the disease, and how you cannot commit someone just because you want to, Tom and I mollified the family. And speaking of the non-violent nature of the disease I explained that violence could be predicted. Dr. Torrey points this out clearly in his book. If the following three factors are present:

History of Violence

Current Drug Abuse, and

No Medication.

John had no history of violence, he was not on street drugs at that time, and he was on heavy medication. (Thank you, Dr. Torrey, you really got me through some tough arguments with the family!) Meanwhile, I was in constant contact with John's doctor and was told I could administer heavy doses of Seroquel until we could get him to the hospital at home.

Before I gave John the heavier doses of Seroquel, one more incident occurred. Armed with a can of bug spray, John approached the same cottage, walked up on the porch and asked for Mary (a former girlfriend). He was afraid that the al Qaeda were holding her there. When the police brought him home once again we were warned that that this was the last time they would deal with John. If there was a next time he would go before a judge and be committed.

With that warning in mind, I watched John every minute of the few days left at the beach until we were to return home. He slept most of the time but when he was awake, I observed how he kept hitting the back of his head, also the sides of his face and neck. He was in constant motion, almost as if something was biting him. Could it be more side effects of Seroquel? The dreaded "Tardive?"

Once, in the middle of the night when he woke up, we sat on the deck and watched "a silent storm at sea" miles away, spectacular lightning playing above a band of clouds and then threading its way down to the ocean, a true fantasy in itself. Sometimes I think that John's illness is all about me. Each day when I think about him and I wonder what I can do to make his life more pleasant, it seems to be more about me and my plans for him. And, just when I think things are going well for him, something always happens.

19

Highs and Lows

HOME AGAIN AND John is hospitalized. He is given Invega, a newer medication with less side effects. I do not see any change in his behavior for a week. He is still angry, anxious, and irritated with the hospital environment.

The first few days, our conversations go like this:

"Why does the fact I mentioned a Russian submarine put me in the hospital?" I answer that we want an evaluation of your illness so that we can go to Hawaii next month and visit Henry and Suzan, his older brother and wife. The promise of a visit to Hawaii had eased the tension of entering the hospital. "By the way, you know I damaged the machine and the voices are lower. Why do I hear these messages? I've had them for too long and now I'm tired of them."

Another comment, "There are too many Russians in Arlington. Why is that? I think Putin and Bush have a secret plan."

"The reason we have this drought here is because there are huge tunnels all over the United States and the Russians are living there taking the rain water."

After six days, John seemed more relaxed and his statements showed this difference:

"You know, sometimes, you shouldn't tell people what you know."

"Who can back me up on what I believed?" My answer was not forthcoming and the silence between us hung like a thick fog (I could not name anyone who could back up John's claims about the

Russians, tunnels, and submarines). No words could penetrate that heavy silence.

On the eighth day, John had definitely improved. He actually smiled at JHS and thanked him for visiting. The improvement was accompanied by John's trying to understand his delusions. He says, "With all the water going into the tunnels and then to the ocean, we should worry more about global tunneling than global warming."

He asks my husband, "Am I crazy to believe this?"

JHS answers that if al Qaeda and 9/11 could happen, anything is possible. And, he adds, "The memories of your delusions are real to you."

So John is released from the hospital after ten days. Dr. Barrara has agreed with us that a direct injection (Risperdal Consta) every two weeks would be far better than the unreliability of taking pills each day. I had read that this is a very common practice in Europe and it made sense to me. With my new understanding of "anosognosia," I give thanks again to Dr. Torrey and TAC (Treatment Advocacy Center) for pointing out to me how John's brain is physically damaged erasing his knowledge of his illness and his need for medication. However, getting the medicine approved presented a challenge but it happened. No more pills. Hurray! John plays Aquarius for me on his old CD player and I relax.

But not for long. Once again when I am thinking everything is going well, we get a call at 6 a.m. from the First District Police Station and we are told that John has been picked up for cocaine possession. After we pick him up, he tells us, "I went to a party in D.C. with a girl. She left. Later, a couple offered to drive me home to Virginia for $20. I climbed in the back seat of their car and within seconds police came up and searched me for cocaine. I was clean but they found a small piece on the floor. Nothing good happens after midnight. I guess I'll be in jail and will not be able to go to Hawaii with you." All I could think of was, here we go again. It is dual diagnosis coming back to haunt me.

Three days before the Hawaii trip, the case was called and dismissed for lack of evidence. As our plane roared down the runway I looked at John and saw his face relax and break into a huge grin. He was going to Hawaii after all.

Returning home after six days and a wonderful time with Henry and Suzan, we settled into the normal routine. John seemed to be hearing voices again, which was, of course, "normal routine." After cleaning the house one day, he told me, "I am listening to the guy walking down the sidewalk outside; he is unlocking all the front doors with his special equipment." Another day he said, "I feel rotten. No money, no driver's license, no job."

I replied, "All that can be fixed" and he agreed. I did not have any idea how that could be fixed but unadulterated "hope" is the only possible alternative I have left.

One morning, John calls and says he cannot clean the house as planned because he is in pain. In D.C. last night, he was knocked to the ground, beaten, and had his wallet and cell phone stolen. While I felt sorry for him, I hoped that this incident would keep him away from D.C. and potential drug dealers. (I was to learn that the dealers exist everywhere and not just in D.C.) Losing his wallet and cell phone was not a new occurrence.

Because of this recent incident, I decided to confront John about using street drugs. He said yes, he had used some when the voices got so loud and unbearable and he felt pain in his body. He was back again self-medicating. He added that he owed some money which he was trying to pay off. If I could lend him some, he would be clear and start all over. He would swear off forever. How many times had I heard this?

I was slowly beginning to realize the truth about John's use of street drugs. It went in cycles, a few hours of street drugs, then, a few months of recovery time while he fought the Schizophrenia and settled his debts. The "recovery" times were lasting longer and longer. During these "recovery" times I would try to get him to movies, museums, or history tours. He would call for job placement interviews. He attended church with every good intention of changing his life style. He even put an ad in the personals, describing himself, hoping to meet somebody. It went like this:

"Handsome SWM (Single, White Male) 44, good guy, kind-hearted, easy-going, low-key attitude, loves nature, history, museums ..."

And a few dates resulted from this.

One morning, John and I visited an outdoor Farm Market. The owner, an older man at the counter, did not respond to my "Good Morning" greeting. He finally looked up and saw John lighting a cigarette.

"That yer son?" he asked.

"Yes," I replied.

"Don't you think you ought to tell him that smoking is bad for him?" he asked. I looked at John, a good distance away and out of earshot, and said firmly, "He has Schizophrenia. I think smoking helps him."

The owner stared at me for a long moment, glanced at John and then started talking non-stop, "These are good vegetables, ma'am, home-grown, very fresh, the tomatoes and especially the corn ... it is good you use environmentally correct bags, and ... and ..." He was still talking as we said goodbye.

I look at John as we walk away. He is very large with muscular biceps, wild hair and a protruding stomach. He grasps his hands together, pressing them fiercely while getting bright red in the face trying to fight the voices by "reducing the body double."It is a scary sight. I am so grateful for the gentle soul which inhabits that large body and for the treatment that he receives. It could be worse, as in the Newtown, Colorado, Tucson, Texas, and Virginia Tech tragedies.

Dr. Torrey, once again,

"It has been estimated that more than 40,000 dangerously mentally ill individuals are roaming America's streets on any given day, untreated...akin to walking time bombs. Why are we so surprised when one occasionally goes off?"

The next incident that occurred was due to my error. John received some money from the Will of a relative. It had been a long "recovery" time and John even gave me some repayment for his debts.

I thought he could handle the rest. Ever the optimist. NO! Not a chance, it was gone within a month. Here I am back again as the good old Enabler! When will I learn? I did hear about a discussion John's siblings had recently about the amount of payoff money going to drug dealers. They had no idea what they would do in a similar situation if it was one of their own children. It seemed it would have to happen to make that decision.

But there was good news forthcoming. John learned through an acquaintance that wonderful Arlington County had a housing program for low-income persons. He applied, and with only his Social Security Disability income to report, within a few months found himself in a new one-bedroom apartment with his very own kitchen and bathroom. What a difference!

20

Not Any More, Or The Book With No End

I DID NOT want to write this last chapter because I didn't know how it would end ... and I have procrastinated for many months. I go to the computer, try to write, and end up playing Spider or Words With Friends (with my family).

The drug dealers have the word on John and they keep coming to his apartment demanding their money or they will "take care of him." He has been threatened with guns, knives, being beat up unless he pays, and because he has owed them money for so long the amount is often doubled.

I wrestle with this problem and what does one do? I have paid and paid but the persistent thought is: am I supporting a habit or am I actually buying John's future as I like to think?

Am I the enabler or the emancipator? Who knows? I don't.

There was a Dr. Phil TV show about parents who cured their son of street drugs by letting him serve six months in jail. During that period of time, the parents seemed to suffer more than their son thinking of all the terrible things that could happen in jail. However, it seemed to work.

Each time John has told me about an old debt he owes, I tell him that I cannot help him any longer ... but then I do. I feel like I am being blackmailed because I do not want any harm to come to John. It is wrong to continue paying off these dealers and I know it. Finally the decision not to help any longer is made by two occurrences: one is the fact that there are no more funds in my tour guide account to help him out. Another factor in ending this cycle of debt is that John swears to me that there are no more dealers looking for him. Even though he has said this to me so many times, I want to believe him. I ask him if he thinks about using street drugs again and he responds with a loud *"Not Any More"*! We will see.

My belief is strengthened by Mother Nature, who intervenes with severe winter snowstorms. The resulting consequence is a three-week period of close association with John. He sprains his ankle the day of the storm and stayed with us for that period of time. We had many long talks and I think he is ready for change in spite of the confusion in his mind. The biggest question I had for him was how he ever expected to pay for the very expensive marijuana or other street drugs? Where did he think the money would come from? His side of the story follows:

"I was convinced that I was going to die. If I was not going to live much longer who would care about the debts? This story goes way back to when I was 19 years old and knew there was something wrong with me. I couldn't figure out what it was. I was hearing many 'people's' mental voices. Much later to my surprise I learned that most of the voices came from a main frame computer as I told you earlier. These 'people' were pressuring me. I could tell that their intentions were not good and at the very same time I began having pains in my body through the wireless electrodes. The pains were so severe that I looked for relief and, as you know, I found it on the streets through cocaine and marijuana. Later, after thousands of electrodes had been planted in me, I understood that these people were actually foreign spies working for the government.

"Do you know what it's like to be followed day and night by the voices? It's impossible to ignore them. They are always with you. There is no time you are alone. It is like an invisible person standing over you giving you thoughts, bad thoughts, not your thoughts. They try to convince me that I am evil and would like to see me dead. I can't act on these thoughts anymore or they'll ruin me."

Is there a glimmer of hope here?

He continues, "I have got to try to live with my problem, the voices from the computer. I must distinguish between my thoughts and the computer voices, and I can do that. I do not want to end up on the street in a shelter."

Just when I think we have reached a new milestone, John asks if I would make a phone call for him. He wants me to call the Secret Service and report that the electrodes placed in his body by a U.S. government computer are making him really sick. He explains to me that when he called recently, the agent who answered the phone asked him if he had taken his medicine that day. Surprisingly, John answered very calmly and said that he had and that the medicine helped him a lot. So that is why he wants me to call. I tell him that I cannot do that. He gets angry with me and says,

"You don't care that I am being killed and you won't do anything about it!"

I reply, "I know this is very real to you but it is not real to me and, also, I have to take a tour group to the State Department on Monday and I might not be admitted if I make that call."

John is upset with me. He tells me that I don't believe him and that he will not talk about the computer any more to me. I am exasperated. And just as I am fretting over this, he comes back to me and says,

"You are right, you cannot do it. I apologize." John continues talking:

"I think now how I've been stuck in the 'moment'. I've never looked forward. If you cannot look forward then street drugs are the answer for the 'moment'. There is no future. But if you can look forward, out of the 'moment', you will be happier because you know there is a future for you."

"What a psychiatrist you have become," I exclaim.

Now I know there is hope for John and it's not just my eternal optimism. Although the voice persecution and the electrodes continue to plague him with delusional beliefs, he is more open to discussing them. One day, as we were watching TV, some of our troops returning from Iraq were labeled with the term PTSD (Post Traumatic Stress Disorder).

"I understand this," he exclaimed. "Stress makes you ill, it creates a poison which damages vital organs in your body, like your brain. I think that's my problem, too."

As we watched, we learned that during the Civil War it was called "Irritable Heart," during World War One it was "Shell Shock," during World War Two it was "Battle Fatigue," and it was known as "Post Viet Nam Syndrome" during that war. So, John is right: stress does cause monstrous damage.

Somehow through all this stress, John has maintained his sense of humor. One day his brother Read called to tell John he had a computer he was not using and asked John if he wanted it.

"No thanks, I am not ready for it," John replied. "I have just begun to walk upright."

* * * *

A year later I understood that John actually had left the 'moment' and was looking to the future. He had proved it. I will never forget the conversation we had over the phone one evening when I was extremely tired from a five day tour with eighth-grade students. I did not feel like talking, much less playing the role of the constant reassurer. Instead, John was reassuring me!

"Everything is working out. You don't have to worry about me any more. I see the future now and I'll have a good life. You relax and get some rest." Was that my son John talking? After all these years? Many more long conversations like this ensued. And, witness, no more drug dealers.

So now I am content to write this last chapter. I tell John that at last

I can finish the book. He is pleased and wants it finished. Does he want me to use his name?

He smiles at me and says, "Yeah, that's me. If the book helps another person who gets caught up in the 'moment' like I did and cannot see the future, then it's worth it. And, I like the title of this last chapter which belongs to me, *Not Any More*.

I think to myself perhaps the book will give him hope. The kind of hope that the voices will cease and the computers/electrodes will shut down.

He is still lonely and he is unable to work but I see his tremendous accomplishments, going from an addicted drug user with severe paranoia to a non-drug user with somewhat less paranoia. He beat the dreaded dual diagnosis.

He still has schizophrenia with the accompanying 'anosognosia'. He believes the electrodes are in his body but he is moving on by ignoring them as much as possible. With the help of treatment his schizophrenia can be contained but not cured.

So, here's to John, the great hero of the book.

ACKNOWLEDGEMENTS

First, the old saying, "I'm between a rock and a hard place" has a different meaning for me. The rock, my husband, John Spaulding, has traveled this long road with me for 31 years with continued patience and understanding.

Second, this book, a family effort, would have been lost without Tom's help and rescue of it, Mary Gregory's superb editing skills, Read's thoughtful suggestions, and the encouragement of friends, Gay, Sheila, Kate, Alexandra, Anneje, Lael and the Monday Lunch Bunch. Many thanks to Editor Arnie, Dr. Torrey and his Treatment Advocacy Center for educating us and to NAMI for all the help they provide to people like us.

CPSIA information can be obtained at www.ICGtesting.com
Printed in the USA
BVOW01s1219040414

349759BV00001B/137/P